797,805 Books

are available to read at

Forgotten Books

www.ForgottenBooks.com

Forgotten Books' App
Available for mobile, tablet & eReader

ISBN 978-1-330-13030-8
PIBN 10033182

This book is a reproduction of an important historical work. Forgotten Books uses state-of-the-art technology to digitally reconstruct the work, preserving the original format whilst repairing imperfections present in the aged copy. In rare cases, an imperfection in the original, such as a blemish or missing page, may be replicated in our edition. We do, however, repair the vast majority of imperfections successfully; any imperfections that remain are intentionally left to preserve the state of such historical works.

Forgotten Books is a registered trademark of FB &c Ltd.
Copyright © 2015 FB &c Ltd.
FB &c Ltd, Dalton House, 60 Windsor Avenue, London, SW19 2RR.
Company number 08720141. Registered in England and Wales.

For support please visit www.forgottenbooks.com

1 MONTH OF FREE READING

at
www.ForgottenBooks.com

By purchasing this book you are eligible for one month membership to ForgottenBooks.com, giving you unlimited access to our entire collection of over 700,000 titles via our web site and mobile apps.

To claim your free month visit: www.forgottenbooks.com/free33182

* Offer is valid for 45 days from date of purchase. Terms and conditions apply.

Similar Books Are Available from
www.forgottenbooks.com

Every Man a King
Or Might in Mind-Mastery, by Orison Swett Marden

Self-Help
With Illustrations of Conduct and Perseverance, by Samuel Smiles

Improvement of the Mind
by Isaac Watts

A Dictionary of Thoughts
by Tryon Edwards

Methods of Obtaining Success
by Julia Seton

The Power of Truth
Individual Problems and Possibilities, by William George Jordan

How to Get What You Want, Vol. 1
by Orison Swett Marden

How to Be Happy Though Married
by Edward John Hardy

Self Development and the Way to Power
by L. W. Rogers

Beginning Right
How to Succeed, by Nathaniel C. Fowler

How to Make Money
Three Lectures on "The Laws of Financial Success", by B. F. Austin

The Pursuit of Happiness
A Book of Studies and Strowings, by Daniel Garrison Brinton

Your Forces, and How to Use Them, Vol. 1
by Prentice Mulford

Conquering Prayer
Or the Power of Personality, by L. Swetenham

He Can Who Thinks He Can, and Other Papers on Success in Life
by Orison Swett Marden

The Power of Thought
What It Is and What It Does, by John Douglas Sterrett

Plenty
by Orison Swett Marden

The Practice of Autosuggestion By the Method of Emile Coué
Revised Edition, by C. Harry Brooks

Thinking for Results
by Christian D. Larson

Calm Yourself
by George Lincoln Walton

Eddie Klimek
13/13 Redbraes Grove
EDINBURGH EH7 4LJ
early.knight@hotmail.co.uk

THE LIBRARY
OF
THE UNIVERSITY
OF CALIFORNIA
LOS ANGELES

Ex Libris

SIR MICHAEL SADLER

ACQUIRED 1948
WITH THE HELP OF ALUMNI OF THE
SCHOOL OF EDUCATION

Edwin Chapman

Small Books on Great Subjects.

Already published.

No. I.
Philosophical Theories and Philosophical Experience. (*Second Edition.*)

No. II.
On the Connection between Physiology and Intellectual Science. (*Second Edition enlarged.*)

No. III.
On Man's Power over Himself to prevent or control Insanity. (*Second Edition enlarged.*)

No. IV.
An Introduction to Practical Organic Chemistry.

No. V.
A Brief View of Greek Philosophy up to the Age of Pericles. (*Second Edition.*)

No. VI.
A Brief View of Greek Philosophy from the Age of Socrates to the Coming of Christ. (*Second Edition.*)

By the same Author,

Pericles, a Tale of Athens in the Eighty-third Olympiad. 2 vols. post 8vo. 18s. (*Longmans and Co.*)

No. VII.
Christian Doctrine and Practice in the Second Century.

No. VIII.
An Exposition of Vulgar and Common Errors adapted to the Year of Grace 1845

No. IX.
An Introduction to Vegetable Physiology, with References to the Works of De Candolle, Lindley, etc.

No. X.
On the Principles of Criminal Law.

No. XI.
Christian Sects in the Nineteenth Century.
(*Second Edition.*)

No. XII.
General Principles of Grammar.

No. XIII.
Sketches of Geology.

No. XIV.
On the State of Man before the Promulgation of Christianity.

No. XV.
Thoughts and Opinions of a Statesman.
(*Second Edition.*)

No. XVI.
On the Responsibilities of Employers.

No. XVII.
Christian Doctrine and Practice in the Twelfth Century.

No. XVIII.
The Philosophy of Ragged Schools.

No. XIX.
Will be published in June
On the State of Man after the Promulgation of Christianity: (*being* Part I. *of the concluding Treatise; it will include the History of Christianity as far as the death of Constantinus Magnus.*)

Small Books on Great Subjects.

EDITED BY A FEW WELL WISHERS

TO KNOWLEDGE.

No. XVIII.

"Non essent igitur hæc omnia in terris mala, si ab universis fierent, quæ unus noster populus operatur. Quam beatus esset quamque aureus humanarum rerum status, si per totum orbem mansuetudo et pietas et pax et innocentia et æquitas et temperantia et fides moraretur! Denique ad regendos homines non opus esset tam multis et tam variis legibus, cum ad perfectam innocentiam Dei lex una sufficeret; neque carceribus, neque gladiis præsidum, neque terrore pœnarum, cum præceptorum cœlestium salubritas humanis pectoribus infusa ultro ad justitiæ opera homines erudiret."—*Lactantius De Justitia.*

THE
PHILOSOPHY OF RAGGED
SCHOOLS

LONDON
WILLIAM PICKERING
1851

THE PHILOSOPHY OF RAGGED SCHOOLS.

Introduction.

IT is but a short time since we were all startled by the news that almost every throne in Christendom had been shaken or overturned by popular insurrection; nor were these insurrections, as on former occasions, headed by persons influential in the State, whom the people followed as their leaders—they were not merely for the subversion of an unpopular party, or the removal of an oppressive law—they aimed at the re-construction of the whole system of society; but where successful, theories so wild were propounded and acted on, that it was at once perceivable that a class of persons very little aware of the duties or the difficulties of government, had for the time taken the management of affairs.

This outbreak of popular discontent, — ay, and this demonstration too, of popular power, which frightened all Europe from its propriety, is just now lulled: but is it quieted altogether? —has military execution sweetened the bitter cup of poverty, or can we expect that a tranquillity so procured will be lasting? This is a question which all ask themselves, from the throne to the cottage: — can any one give a satisfactory answer? — Even while the writer is preparing these sheets for the press, events may solve the problem, and then, will England, whose anchors held firm during the strain of the last storm, ride out another equally well? The question is no light one, and deserves, not *more* attention, but *wiser* attention than has yet been bestowed upon it.

There are few probably who have not of late years become aware that the state of society is not a healthy one: that there is much of misery and vice, and of luxury and vice also in such close juxta position, that it can hardly fail to awaken discontent in the class which is subjected to the rigour of the law for offences of no deeper dye, though different in kind, from those daily perpetrated by persons of the so-called *better* classes. Furthermore, it has become painfully apparent that when these discontents reach a certain pitch, revolutions very distasteful to those better and higher classes, are apt to take place. All this is well known, and a variety of remedies have from time to time been proposed for the social evils whose existence all acknowledge. Ireland was groaning under the effects of ignorance and faction: " Give us Catholic Emancipation," cried certain demagogues, and the cry was echoed by the people. Some persons ventured to suggest that whatever might be the abstract justice of the demand, the country was suffering from other evils than those produced by the disability to sit in Parliament, which prevented some thirty or forty gentlemen of the Romish faith from lending their aid to the national councils. These unenthusiastic persons, however, were disregarded;—" Catholic Emancipation " was the one thing needful:—*that* would quiet all disturbances, make a lawless population obedient to their rulers, and fill a starving people with bread. It was given; what followed? Were the evils of Ireland cured? On the contrary; they have increased ten fold; and the coffers of England have been drained to supply food for its famishing inhabitants, perishing under the consequences of the very evils which Catholic Emancipation was vainly expected to cure.*

There was much in England which called for amendment: and with a like confidence "Parliamentary Reform" was held out as the panacea which would cure all evils. The people figured to themselves all sorts of impossible benefits which they were to derive from it, and were ready to rise in insurrection to force on "the hill, the whole hill, and nothing but the hill;" not because they recognized its principle, but because they were anxious to clutch these visionary advantages. The bill passed:—what did the masses gain by it? Their own answer may be heard now by those who choose to ask them; and with a frowning brow, and a bitter sneer, they reply—" Nothing."

Another political nostrum quickly followed this:—a New Poor Law was to do everything;

---

* At the time when the above measure was in progress, the writer was in company with a Member of the House of Commons who was one of its strenuous supporters. "Now is your time to lay out your money to advantage," said he, " land is comparatively cheap now in Ireland on account of the disturbed state of the country. When this bill is passed, estates will be double in value, and if I had £20,000 to lay out I would become an Irish proprietor." The state of Ireland for many years past forms the best comment on this too sanguine prophecy.

the poor's rates were weighing down the energies of the country, and fostering crowds of sturdy idle labourers: " the workhouse test" was to set everything right, and it would soon be found that a man, with a wife and seven children, could maintain all upon the average wages of from ten to twelve shillings per week, even though the increasing extent of grass land left agricultural labourers frequently without work during many weeks. Workhouses arose every where, stately, and vast, and prison-like; outdoor relief was prohibited, and no doubt was entertained that the poor were at once to become well conducted, contented, and happy. What was the result? The alternative offered to the honest and industrious labourer was either starvation, or entrance into the Union Workhouse; where every dear domestic tie was at once torn asunder: where the children were separated from parents whose small mental resources generally render the family bond closer, and even more essential to comfort than among the rich: where the husband was placed among the idle and the reprobate; the wife among the dissolute of her own sex. They left the workhouse, probably, when summer work began; but were they what they were when they entered it? That law has been amended since, or perhaps England, like France, might have witnessed another servile war; but the spirit which pervaded originally, and in which it was first administered, has branded its mark deeply in the wounded feelings of the poor.

Again a cry has been raised: the corn laws, it was said, stood in the way of the comforts of the poorer classes: they have been abolished; but the most sanguine of the Free Trade party has not seen, nor will he ever see accomplished the great results which he imagined were to follow.

What next?—are we to have a new nostrum every Session or two to cure the diseases of the body politic, like the quackeries which are depended ou with equal faith in the cure of the diseases of the body natural, and which sometimes leave things worse, never better, than they were before? Œconomical Reform; the Five Points of the Charter; a Paper Currency; the Abolition of the Irish Church Establishment; all have their supporters; none of whom yield to the others in the magniloquence of their talk, while descanting on the wonders of their specifics; yet in the mean time, there the poor patient lies, dosed with course after course of new medicines of which no one can guess the effect, while not a man among them all has the skill to find out the real seat of the disease. There is danger, great and imminent danger; and statesmen and legislators allow it: yet they dally with it, give an opiate here, and a cordial there, and trust to the *vis medicatrix* of good dame Nature.

Constant failure ought to have taught us more wisdom, and by shewing us where the evil *is not*, have brought us near the cause of the disease which is eating away the very life of our social system; for as in the body natural the illnesses which follow time after time upon exposure to cold, bad diet, insufficient ventilation, &c. are so many lessons to teach us the necessity of prudent care; so in the body politic, discontent among our poor, crime, revolutions, are so many symptoms of disease whose causes ought to be sought out and removed, if we would enjoy a state of health and comfort.

There was a time when pestilences were considered as immediate and inscrutable judgments of the Almighty, inflicted on guilty nations for their sins: advancing science has taught us to modify that opinion, and we perceive that they result from disregard of those great physical laws to which the Creator has subjected all material things. It is often a guilty disregard it is true, as in cases where disease is caused by ignorance or misery which it is in the power of the higher and more educated classes to remove; and these last suffer a deserved punishment in sharing the danger with those neglected poor, among whom the seeds of disease have sprung up unheeded. The scourge, therefore, comes *mediately* not *immediately* from the Almighty; it might be avoided; and man inflicts on himself the punishment of his perverseness or his neglect. And thus it is also in regard to the moral laws of the universe: revolutions are not more direct inflictions from above than pestilences; they have been prepared long before, by a course of neglect or infraction of those great laws whose object is the happiness of all; and as surely as fever follows upon the breathing tainted air, so surely will crime and insurrection follow upon the misgovernment which allows any class to grow up amid a moral taint, no less fatal to the spiritual, than the former to the animal part, of man.

Much has been said and written on criminal law, and on " secondary punishments :"—" penitentiaries," "solitary confinement," the "silent system," &c. have been vaunted by their respective supporters as unfailing specifics; but the result of all has nevertheless been an increase of crime in the course of this century far more than commensurate with the increase of population; and our rulers still avow themselves in the dark as to the best means of disposing of our criminals; but it does not seem to have occurred to any one that if a criminal population be so troublesome, so dangerous to our colonies, and so expensive at home; it would be far better to prevent than to punish. We all know that crime is comparatively rare in country places, and that it is only in populous cities that it becomes rampant. " A London thief" is a master of his business; and a policeman will detect in an instant the hand of an expert and practised London burglar in the manner of breaking into a house: but no one seems to have considered that in order to become perfect there must be a teaching, with frequent practice superadded; and that if our criminal records are filled from the pupils of one great school, the best, and probably the only way of lessening the number of convictions, would be to break up if possible this seminary of vice. It is a conviction of this which has led a few, — too few, — benevolent persons to endeavour, ere it be too late, to counteract the mischief, and arrest the progress of the moral pestilence whose very magnitude has hitherto prevented the attempt. Hence the establishment of " RAGGED SCHOOLS."

Let those who may be disposed to doubt the expediency or the success of a movement begun by humble tradesmen, overlooked, or perhaps scorned by the great and the wealthy, remember that the world was once in a worse state than now, the rich more licentious, the poor far more wretched and corrupt ; and who then undertook its reform, and in great measure accomplished it? — Eleven poor men, one of the middling class, and one gentleman and scholar! Though opposed and despised by the proud and the great, and too often maltreated by the wretched beings whose condition they strove to amend, " through evil report and good report," they did effect a change of thought and feeling which has been propagated to the farthest regions of the earth, and is still animating the true believers of the blessed law then taught, to walk in the steps of their first Great Master,* and to carry

---

* I know nothing more touching than the answer of one of those worthy tradesmen to a person who asked him who was at their head — " We have no head, Sir,

INTRODUCTION. 11

the message of peace to the hearts of the wretched.

The danger to society at large from the unhappy class which for the first time has found care and sympathy from the teachers of the Ragged Schools, has been seen and recognized in other countries also: so long ago as 1840, a work was published at Paris, by M. Fregier, on the dangerous classes of the population in great cities, and the methods of ameliorating them,† which had its origin in a question proposed by

---

we are all servants of One Master." A reply worthy of the time when Peter and the other Apostles stood before the Sanhedrim, and avowed themselves the undaunted preachers of that doctrine which was " to the Jews a stumbling-block, and to the Greeks foolishness." It was the blood of such men, shed like water in the service of that *One Master*, which was, as an ancient Christian writer expresses it, the *Semen Christianorum* which grew up into so rich a harvest.

† " Voici les termes mêmes de la question mise au concours par l' Acadèmie des sciences morales et politiques: Rechercher d'après des observations positives, quels sont les élémens dont se compose à Paris, ou dans toute autre grande ville, cette partie de la population qui forme une classe dangereuse par ses vices, son ignorance et sa misère ; indiquer les moyens, que l'administration, les hommes riches ou aisés, les ouvriers intelligens et laborieux pourraient employer pour améliorer cette classe dangereuse et depravée. " Des Classes dangereuses." Avant propos.

the Academy of Moral and Political Sciences; and in that year M. M. Demetz and Bretignieres established an asylum at Mettray, intended for the reformation of young criminals, on somewhat the same plan as our Philanthropic Society: other establishments of the same kind are to be found in France, as well as in other countries, but every where there is the same radical fault; the reformation is not attempted till some overt act of a criminal nature has been committed, and the boy is become amenable to the laws. The simple, and one would have thought, very obvious plan, of breaking up the great training school of vice, by instructing and reclaiming these outcasts of society before they have become adepts in the arts of villany, never seems to have occurred to any till a few years back. The insurrections and slaughters which have deluged with blood almost every great city in Europe, have formed a fearful comment on the mistakes and neglects of governments.

There is an extraordinary disinclination in most minds to search to the bottom of things: in the natural sciences, indeed, we begin to see that a few simple principles form the groundwork of all knowledge; and he who takes the phænomenon as it is, without inquiring into its causes, is considered to have forfeited all claim to scientific distinction; but in politics it is far otherwise: there none look for the first principles on which all law or government must be founded, if it is to be either permanent in itself, or advantageous to mankind; and the emergencies of the day are, for the most part, met by expedients of a no less ephemeral character. A law is repealed, perhaps, which seems to have caused discontent; or another made, about which popular clamour has been raised; but he who should go back to those moving springs of human action which ought to be thought of whenever legislation is attempted, would be held an impracticable visionary by every statesman in Europe; and would be told that "practical men" cannot lose their time over theories. These eminently practical men, nevertheless, have found their task of governing nations grow year by year, more onerous — year by year the prospect grows darker, and none seem now able to see their way at all clearly before them. There must be a fault in the system when this is the case; and as surface treatment has not succeeded, perhaps they will begin at last to see that a different plan may possibly be better. Let us see if there be not some clear and simple principles which may avail us in political, no less than in natural science.

Although in strictness every step of an argument should be proved, I shall not undertake to demonstrate here what none of our statesmen deny, namely, the being of a God, and a future state of existence, because it is to be concluded that what a man professes to believe has been sufficiently demonstrated to his mind to satisfy him of its truth: and if sufficiently demonstrated to satisfy him of its truth, then it necessarily becomes a motive when he is called upon to act in any matter connected with it. Our statesmen, then, generally acknowledge, as certain, the two above-mentioned great facts; but have they in their legislation kept them in view? If every one born into the world has the possibility of a happy immortality granted him, but which may be lost by his own misconduct, and if legislators believe this, is it possible to justify the neglect with which they treat the great bulk of the people in regard to this, their greatest privilege? Their thews and sinews are wanted for the industrial progress of the nation, says the Statesman—Granted: we will for the present drop the question as to whether the mind can be cultivated while the hands are employed in mechanical or agricultural occupations : but if it really were necessary that in order to the industrial progress of a nation, nine-tenths of its population should be doomed to ignorance and the vices most usually consequent upon ignorance,* and legislators resolutely attend to the industrial, and slide carelessly over the moral progress of the people what is the inevitable conclusion ? It is vain to shrink, and blind ourselves to the discrepancy between our avowed belief and our actions; for if the actions do not tally with this avowed belief, either we must be under coercion, and unable to act voluntarily ; or the belief which we profess to entertain is a mere mockery— words repeated without thought, which have never come from the heart, and which if we have the least vestige of respect for truth remaining, ought never to be uttered again. I repeat then, if it were necessary to the prosperity of the nation that nine-tenths of its population should be

---

* Let me not be supposed to cast this censure on all without discrimination, the intellectual rights of the masses have been recognised and ministered to by several of our statesmen, but they have not been strong enough to stem the current setting the other way ; and it is doubtful whether even they serve the full importance of the question in a moral point of view.

abandoned to ignorance and vice, and if at the same time we believe truly that all these persons have a happy immortality within their reach, which they will lose by misconduct, could the question as to which ought to have the first place in our consideration, be entertained for a moment? Every man who felt this conviction would necessarily say, "Let us give as far as in us lies a happy immortality to these myriads of persons born with a capability for this blessed lot;—the number of bales of cotton imported, or of vessels fraught with the produce of our manufactories or our mines, can only be a secondary thought.[*] Will no one say or feel this? Then no one in his heart believes in such an immortality: and it is better at once to tear away the covering,

---

[*] Let it however be here observed that this is only a proposition assumed for the sake of showing the inconsistency of our legislators and rulers: for the progress of a nation towards greatness is usually commensurate with its moral and religious earnestness. The impetus given by a better spirit may carry on a generation or two to apparent greatness, as we have seen in most great empires; but if the standard of morality be low, and the religious feeling extinct or languid, the downfall of that empire is approaching. This subject has been admirably treated in a small work lately published, entitled "Social Aspects. By John Stores Smith."

and shew in broad day light the secret unbelief which, like a canker, is eating into the core of our social system; for, if I mistake not, it is this which vitiates all our legislation, and, though unavowed, shews its results in our habits of thought and action. The belief repeated with the lips is a thing apart,—the real belief which lies at the bottom and regulates the whole, is, that for a nation no less than an individual, *wealth is the* SUMMUM BONUM; and that nothing else can constitute real well-being: if, in addition to this, an immortality of happiness can be obtained, it is well; but if not—still get wealth, and enjoy the greatness and luxury it affords to the few:—the want, the vice, the ignorance of the many need not be thought of yet: and every fresh generation says the same thing, till the many become too many and too strong for the few; and then, trained to believe that wealth and its attendant luxuries form the sole good, they enact, in grosser and more revolting excess, the only practical lesson which the world has ever taught them.

This assuredly is not such a result as political wisdom would seek, and even the most short sighted rulers, where the danger is imminent, strive to avert it; but this is generally done by severe enactments, or military execution; which may perhaps preserve peace by means of terror, but which leave the evil not only unremedied, but increasing; inasmuch as the submission of fear lasts no longer than the force which causes it is overpowering; and this is an unsafe principle to depend upon. The question proposed by the French Institute shows how little progress has been made in the great science of government, even after twenty-six years of comparative quiet: since, in spite of the apparent prosperity of the nation, the numbers of persons composing the dangerous classes were great enough to excite apprehensions which subsequent events too fatally justified, and the revelations of many of the actors in the recent scenes, leave us no doubt as to the motives and feelings of those who set Europe in a ferment two years ago. "How is that part of the population which in Paris and other great cities is dangerous to the peace of society by its vices, its ignorance, and its poverty, to be amended by the government or the upper classes?" This is the question proposed; has it yet received a satisfactory answer, either in England or elsewhere? I think not; and if this be the case,—if legislators and statesmen virtually confess their incapacity by applying only empirical and temporary remedies to so rooted an evil in the body politic, it affords a strong ground for suspecting that the whole system is a vicious one, and that the fundamental principles of all government, which can only be fixed by a deep knowledge of the nature of the beings to be ruled, are as yet mistaken at least, if not disregarded. In this state of things, with a danger great and imminent, and a government unable or unwilling to grapple with it, it is not wonderful that individuals who think they can see a remedy, should step forward to make the experiment; and if that experiment be, as it has proved itself in most instances, eminently successful, it is still less wonderful that it should have attracted the attention of the editors of the present series. Perhaps, even to the worthy persons who have set hand and heart to the work, the deeper causes of their success have hardly been apparent; for, to their credit, not their disparagement, let it be said, it was not among the great or the learned that it originated. Christian benevolence supplied the place of philosophy and science; but it can be displeasing to none, and may be useful to many, to shew that philosophy and science dictate the same course. We are not ashamed to have learned from the Carpenter's son,—so his countrymen styled him when they meant to disparage his teaching,—let us not now be ashamed to take another lesson from men in the same rank of life, and acknowledge that where the "disputer of this world" has now, as formerly, been at fault, they, in their simple following of their One Master, have found the path to safety and happiness for all, were it but possible to persuade others to pursue a like course with the same hearty devotion to the good of their fellow creatures, and the will of their Lord.

CHAPTER I.

The dangerous Classes.

THE very title of this chapter is, perhaps, the severest reproach which could be made to a government; for, undoubtedly, the object of all government deserving the name, ought to be that the people should be at once free and happy:—free to do all that is not detrimental to the general happiness; free to enjoy the rational and moderate gratification of the needs of our common nature, and wise enough to be satisfied with this moderate gratification. If indeed any should suffer their animal passions to overpower their reason so far as to seek their gratification at the expense of others, then social law steps in, and forbids violence under pain of punishment; but at the same time says, "return to the path you have forsaken, and we offer you whatever is *needful* to human nature." This is a good government: and this is the beau ideal of the English law and constitution :—the good government for which many a field has been fought over, and grown rich with the blood of those who poured it out freely for the cause they supported. For this, too, France has seen tens of thousands of her inhabitants sacrificed; and thought, after each sanguinary revolution, that the good government was at last attained. Why then have France and England " Dangerous Classes," numerous and formidable enough to make it a question in the one country, of how long a government can exist at all in the presence of such an organised discontent? in the other, of how long a time may elapse before the same classes may rise to the same power? There is, however, this difference, that in France a large body of its legislators and people altogether ignore any future state of existence, and it is apparently no blot on a man's character to do so; in England it is bad taste to avow any such sentiment, and whatever indifference there may be in the heart, the lips must profess a belief in a God and an hereafter. I shall have occasion farther on to recur to this difference.

The Dangerous Classes in England, no less than in France, consist of those whom vice or poverty, or ignorance—generally all three— have placed in a state of warfare with social order. Society has done nothing for them, and they are soured and brutalized. When persons in this state of mind become numerous, there is always danger;—first, to individuals, from isolated acts of violence, and next, to the state, from their combined action: but, as is well observed by M. Fregier, in the work already mentioned, the law can do little or nothing in this matter;* for

---

* "Dans les grandes villes et surtout a Paris la police ne peut exercer une surveillance assez directe ni assez étendue pour avoir action sur les individus qui ont coutume de mener une vie déréglée. Il faudrait qu'elle disposât de légions d'agens, et ceux qui connaissent les ressorts de cette grande et utile machine autrement que par les préjugés vulgaires, savent que ses moyens d'action sont très bornés en raison de l'immense population de Paris. D'ailleurs, la police a pour mandat de poursuivre les faits qualifiés contravention, délit, ou crime, par la loi pénale; et le vice proprement dit n'est pas punissable toutes les fois qu'il reste en dehors des prévisions de cette loi. . . . L'administration est désarmée en presence de l'homme vicieux, tantque ses excès ne tendent pas à troubler la paix de la cité. Elle ne peut juger de la corruption des différentes classes d'ouvriers que par les faits qui tombent sous sa jurisdiction; et ces faits, encores qu'ils aient leur source dans les desordres d'une mauvaise vie, ne forment qu'une faible partie de ceux que l'honnêteté publique réprouve."—*Fregier. Des Classes Dangereuses.* tom. i. p. 29.

If this be so in Paris, with how much more justice may the same observation be applied to London, where the population is so much more numerous.

that can only take cognisance of acts which invade the rights of others, and thus lead to the disturbance of social order; and the Dangerous Classes only send their representatives into our prisons and courts of law, but are by no means to be found there in their entirety.

It is impossible to arrive at the statistics of crime·—we only hear of it when it shows itself in public acts; but every one may make his own statistics on this head, by examining, as closely as he can, into the characters of those he is acquainted with. The general result will be, that in England we shall find the great majority externally decent in their conduct, but without any really settled principle to guide them;—a few incorrigibly vicious,—a few upright and virtuous. It requires no great penetration to know that, where there is no fixed principle, the individual is at the mercy of every temptation; and hard labour, poverty, and ignorance, place far greater temptations before him than ever are felt by those whose exercise never exceeds the bounds of pleasure, whose wants are abundantly supplied, and whose mind has been enough cultivated to supply amusement for leisure. The labourer is in a far different state from this; his strength, if not exhausted, is worn by a day's work—a stimulus under such circumstances is agreeable, at any rate;—the man is not aware that the organs may be injured by such stimuli as he knows how to apply, and he has never been taught self-government;—a first glass is pleasure, and then comes the craving for a repetition of it, till he has spent on drink what should have afforded him and his family food. His master, with less temptation, drinks as much, and without the same cause for it; but *he can afford it,* and no one complains: the poor man knows this, and when he is taunted and lectured on his habit of spending his money at the beer and spirit shop, he thinks of it;—says nothing, probably, but passes into the class of secretly discontented persons who would care little if an order of things were upset under which they think they have suffered injustice. Even his ignorance, which leaves him no means of amusement or pleasure but such as arise from the gratification of animal desires, render him far more open to temptation on this side than his master:—yet, must we pursue the hateful parallel farther? A poor man, uninstructed, and consequently gross in his views and feelings, in the heat of passion, transgresses, but marries the woman who has been the partner of his wrong doing: a large family ensues, and he is without work; and when he asks for relief he is sent to the workhouse, where he is separated from his wonted companions, and drags on his hours wearily and discontentedly. Does he not recollect that the "gentlemen" at the board of guardians have perhaps many of them so transgressed, and have *not* married the woman thus injured? that they have merely paid for, not repented of these sins?—And another is added to the Dangerous Class.

But if those who thus brood over the wrongs they have received from society, be dangerous, is it not also dangerous to have a class above them who show by their example that *respectability*—the "unspiritual god" of the English—does not depend on purity and benevolence of heart and manners, but on a sufficient portion of wealth to supply selfish indulgences without trenching on the general appearance to the eyes of the world? A man who by fraud can rise to affluence, is immediately most highly respectable; his fraud is discovered, and fails of producing riches;—he has the same desires, the same unscrupulousness, but he is poor; he robs to obtain money, spends it in vicious indulgences, robs again, and becomes one of the dangerous class. Is he better in the one situation than in the other? and is it not equally hazardous to the well-being of society to have a numerous body ready on the least change of circumstances to enter the dangerous classes? The evil then lies deeper than we are willing to allow; and if we would avoid a catastrophe like that of France, we must remember that it is not the lower class alone that requires amelioration.

Vice, like war, feeds itself: for from the vices of the parents spring up a race of wretched children, illegitimate, abandoned altogether, or actually trained to wickedness, who in their turn swell the ranks of these so-called dangerous classes. These children, in great cities like London or Paris, maintain themselves for the most part by petty thefts, and thus levy a large tax on the community. Houses of entertainment for these unfortunates are found profitable, and the fruits of robbery are spent in coarse and vicious indulgences. In London, under the title of *Gaffs*, a rude sort of theatrical entertainment is given, where one penny only is charged for admission; the subjects are chosen

from the adventures of thieves, &c. and the language is suited to the subject and the hearers.*
The play bills of these theatres are written, not

---

* The following are specimens of the dialogue in these pieces.

Enter *Tom Snook, Henry Finch, and Ned Jones.*

Tom. I say, Harry, will you lend me a tanner (sixpence) till to-morrow.

Finch. I would if I could, but blow me tight if I've got one.

Tom. I say, chaps! as we are all poor alike, what do you say to agoin' a robbin some old rich fellows?

Finch. Capital, Tom, nothing could be better. Don't you think so, Ned? &c. . . . . .

Ned. I say chaps, hush! I'm blowed if there be not an old fellow in the road there. Let's begin with him.

Tom. Done Ned, done!

Finch. Come Ned, may I never have a button to my coat if you ben't a regular trump!

Enter *a Stranger.*

Stranger. Can you tell me, friends, how far it is to the next inn?

Ned (seizing him by the throat). Your money or your life, sir!

Tom. Yes, my old *bowl,* your money or your life?

Finch. And this moment too.

Stranger. Oh, oh! that's it is it; but how do you know I've got any?

Ned. Then out goes your brains *(putting his hand be-*

printed, and the title of one of the pieces may give some notion of the species of entertainment.

---

neath a sort of cloak as if grasping a pistol in his hand.)

Stranger. Why my good friends, if the truth must be told, I'm quite as destitute of brains as of money. I've got none of either.

Ned. Come, old fellow, no gammon with us. If you don't fork out the yellow boys (sovereigns) presently I'll send a ball through your carcase which will make a passage large enough to let a coach and six be driven through with ease.

Stranger. You don't mean that?

Ned. We do indeed.

Here the appearance of some persons puts an end to the dialogue, and the three thieves take to their heels. Shortly afterwards they reappear on the stage in a jocular mood, and converse on various subjects as follows:

Tom. They say the cholera is coming to wisit the town.

Finch. Vell, and vat about it?

Ned. Vy should they let it come into the town?

Tom. But how can they keep it out?

Ned. Vy, by giving the toll-keeper strict orders not to let it pass the turnpike gate on any account," &c.

The actors, however, for the most part say and do what they like in these pieces. Thrusting and stabbing in the tragic pieces, slapping one another's faces, and pulling one another's caps over the eyes in the farces, form the usual accompaniments.

"On Thursday next will be performed at Smith's Grand Theatre,
The Red-nosed Monster"
or
The Tyrant of the Mountain.

Characters,

The Red-nosed Monster.
The Assassin.
The Ruffian of the Hut.
The Villain of the Valley.
Wife of the Red-nosed Monster.
Daughter of the Assassin.

To conclude with
The "Blood stained Handkerchief"
or
The Murder in the Cottage.

The Characters by the Company.

In some parts of London these houses, which are of course unlicensed, have been put down as nuisances; but a large number remain, some of them of considerable size. One, in Paddington, is calculated to hold two thousand persons. "The audience of these places," says a spectator, "consists almost exclusively of the youthful part of the community. . Youths from eight to sixteen years of age are the great features of such places. There is a tolerable sprinkling of girls, but usually the boys considerably preponderate.

"No one who has not visited these establishments could have the faintest conception of the intense interest with which boys in the poorer neighbourhoods of London regard them. With thousands the desire of witnessing the representations at the Penny Theatres amounts to an absolute passion. There can be no question that these places are no better than so many nurseries of juvenile thieves * plans for

---

* The following instances taken from the Report of the Inspector of Prisons, farther show the temptations to which children and youths of the lowest classes in London are exposed. J. H. aged eighteen. "I had just entered the fifth year of my apprenticeship, and was to receive seven shillings a week, which had been raised from half-a-crown. I read 'Jack Sheppard' about five months before I began the robberies. I saw 'Jack Sheppard' played twice, it excited in my mind an inclination to imitate him. The part was well acted at the play. I read how he got into places, and I had a wish to do the same. *The play made the greatest impression on my mind.* A few weeks after I saw the play, I committed the first robbery."

J. C. seventeen. "The first beginning of my bad conduct was seeing a play acted at the theatre the play was about a highwayman, so we thought we would

thieving, and robbing houses and shops, are there formed, and speedily executed."

"The number of children frequenting low theatres is almost incredible;" says one of the Inspectors of prisons, "the streets in front, and the avenues leading to them may be seen, in the nights of performance, occupied by crowds of boys who have not been able to possess themselves of the few pence required to obtain admission. I will describe as a sample, one place of amusement, called the 'Penny Hop,' to which the admission is one penny, and where two or three series of performances take place the same evening. It consists of a spacious room, fitted up in the rudest manner, with a stage, and seats on an inclined plane, the access to it is through a dark passage, and up a ladder staircase. On one occasion I was present, and found the audience to consist almost exclusively *of boys and girls of the very lowest description*, many without shoes or stockings, and to the number of 150. I pointed out to the superintendant of

---

try to do as he did." Another lad says "I noticed them picking one another's pockets upon the stage. It gave me a great insight into how to do it." Among ninety boys examined, most of them declared that they had stolen money to see " Jack Sheppard" performed.

Police (who accompanied me) a well-dressed youth among the number, who proved to be the son of a respectable tradesman, and he was delivered over to his parents. I had some conversation with the persons in the interior, who appeared to have the management, and they stated, in answer to my queries, that the theatre was almost always filled, and with boys; that they had attempted to play 'Jack Sheppard,' but in consequence of the frequent interruptions from the audience (who seemed all to wish to take a part in the performance) they were obliged to give it up."* The report goes on to observe, " the flaunting exterior of these shows attract crowds of children about them in the evenings, and must be added to the already too numerous temptations in the markets and streets. Nor are the objects represented of that innocent and elevating character which should mark the amusements of those of younger years. If they do not directly corrupt the mind, they tend to its vitiation, by familiarizing it with scenes of grossness, crime, and blood, all represented with a revolting coarseness. The murder of Maria in the Red Barn by Corder, of Hannah Brown

---

* Sixth Report of Prisons, p. 123.

by Greenacre, and other similar atrocities, are among the most common exhibitions." The low theatres, shows, penny hops, &c. are found to be the proximate cause of ruin in fifty-two cases out of the ninety, and connected more or less with the practice of crime in others.*

This may be true; but these places of assemblage would have no existence if there were not previously a class of persons likely to be visitors; and though where a nursery of evil is thus established, it may carry corruption among those, who, having no mental principles at all, are at the mercy of every temptation; still these are not the causes but the effects of a seething corruption which here finds vent; and the suppression of these would do very little more towards the cure, than an endeavour to suppress the eruption of the small pox, otherwise than by lessening the fever which causes it. The moral fever no doubt will leave ugly spots and scars upon the face of society; but it is only by alleviating the disease, of which these things are but the symptomatic eruption, that the evil can be lessened. It is not, therefore, by suppressing penny Gaffs, or Flash houses, that we shall mend

---

* Sixth Report of Prisons, p. 123.

the " Dangerous Classes," but by preventing the growth of that portion of the population which forms their constantly increasing strength. Youth can be bent by instruction, and it was to the credit of that government of France which is now overthrown, that, under it, an enlightened attempt was made to meet the danger by the true remedy. The following account of the salles d'asile in Paris might afford useful hints for London.

" The *salles d'asile* have been established solely for children of the poorer classes. They are designed for the cultivation of the growing intelligence, and the religious and moral instruction of a considerable number of children of from two to seven years of age." The style of teaching seems to resemble that of our infant schools with this difference, that a meal or meals seemed to be provided for them.*

---

* " L' institution des Salles d'asile est due à la necessité de protéger la première enfance contre l'abandon, l'incurie des parens, et contre les accidens de toutes sortes auxquels elle est exposée, par suite de l'impossibilité ou ces mêmes parens se trouvent quelquefois de les surveiller, en raison des exigences de leur profession. Les classes pauvres et laborieuses sont, en effet, tellement commandées par les nécessités du travail dont elles tirent leur subsistence ainsi que celle de leur famille, qu'il y aurait

"The restlessness natural to their age **not** allowing the masters and mistresses to require them to fix their attention long on the same thing, they are led from one occupation to another, so as not to fatigue them, till the hour for meals or recreation: and this well arranged distribution of business and pleasure makes the asylum very pleasant to them. Many of these halls in Paris contain from an hundred to an hundred and fifty children; that in the *rue de l'Homme armé* is the most remarkable, on account of the extreme indigence of the parents who take their children thither, and the variety of their religious opinions. There **are** many Jews mixed with Christians, and **notwithstanding** the different creeds of their relations, as the religious ideas inculcated are those merely of the knowledge and love of God, no conscience is

---

de l'injustice a ni pas peser cette circonstance indépendante de leur volonté, dans l'appréciation de la conduite qu'ils tiennent à l'ègard de leur enfans. Cependant quelque opinion que l'on puisse avoir de la situation de ceux-ci avant l'ouverture des salles d'asile, toujours est il que l'hospitalité qui leur est offerte par la cité dans ces établissemens, constitue pour eux une véritable assurance contre les dangers de toute espèce auxquels ils étoient exposés avant la réalisation d'un projet aussi simple, et dont la première pensée a été si tardive."—FRECIER *des Classes Dangereuses*, tom. ii. p. 6.

offended ... The salles d'asile are under the inspection of a committee of ladies, to whom the warmest thanks are due, since from the moment that the municipal administration took charge of these establishments, they have watched over them with a zeal and care which have never for a moment relaxed. This committee now forms a necessary part of the establishment, and indeed, who are so fit to watch over so fragile and delicate a deposit as the mothers of families, when animated by a disinterested benevolence? who better than they can bestow the kindness and attention which childhood stands so much in need of? Paid teachers and inspectors would not bring to their functions the same moral energy, the same warm and gentle charity.

We have remarked that the children in these asylums belong to the lowest classes, the ladies charged with their inspection, on the contrary, occupy a high rank in society; they have leisure, they have wealth, or at least a competent fortune. Their functions are not confined to the watching over the intellectual and moral state of the pupils; they hear from the chiefs of the establishment all the wants, not only of the children, in regard to clothing, but also those of the parents who may be in extreme poverty. Not unfrequently these ladies themselves carry their benevolent assistance to the homes of the wretched. . . . . . .

" These salles d'asile are amongst the most useful and popular institutions of our time. In a great part of the manufacturing towns, where the municipality have had the wisdom to establish them, the workmen, after a short hesitation, have seen the advantage, and have sent their children. And there is this special benefit arising from these establishments, — i. e. that the children who were many of them prematurely employed in the manufactories, now gain strength of constitution no less than intellectual and moral culture, during their attendance there .... If public benevolence," adds M. Frégier, from whose account the foregoing is abridged, " can ever be applied with success to the moral amendment of the people, it will certainly be by active concurrence in the establishment and multiplication of these asylums, no less by gifts than by advice. One of the most essential and urgent questions of social œconomy is that which has for its object the fixing the legal age at which children may be employed in the manufactories, without injury to their health or their morals; or at least, in the way that shall lessen the injury to the utmost degree possible. This question has a manifest connection with the establishment of *Salles d'asile,* since these have for their special object the preserving children from such dangers as they incur in great industrial establishments, where they are admitted too early: and this object is not merely of interest to the children of the poor, but to the State itself, which ought to watch with the utmost solicitude over the means of preserving the strength of the population, and the purity of its morals." *

When we consider what would be the advantages of such establishments in England, we feel tempted to ask, why, with all our riches and activity, none have yet taken a lesson from our neighbour country, and accomplished a like work of benevolence? which, were it extensively adopted, would change the whole face of the social system, and by the time a generation so trained grew up, would nullify all fears about the dangerous classes. We shall see farther on what has been done by private exertions: but this is too great a work to be trusted to individual benevolence alone, and if, in the room of casual relief to the poor, that relief were steadily

---

* Frégier, des Classes Dangereuses, tom. ii. p. 6.

given in the shape of two sufficient meals to the children sent to these schools, they would not be kept away whenever they could earn a **few** pence; and they would have been trained to habits of right conduct at a time when the **absolute** character is formed: for it is a fact well known among physiologists, that the brain, on whose due developement the character of the individual in great measure depends, is in the course of growth during the first seven years, and the impressions made at this time may be said to be made for life. If, therefore, good habits can then be given, the after task is easy. Many a teacher of Sunday and other schools, has had to complain of the difficulty he experienced in awakening any thing like thought in minds stiffened in ignorance; but could we suppose the very young children of the poor brought into constant exercise of their faculties, a very different result might be expected; and how could our ladies of rank and fortune, in town or country, be better employed than in a work at once so christian, and so patriotic? On what principle such instruction should be conducted, we shall consider by and by. At present our business is only with the possible means of lessening a danger which all acknowledge. The

Salles d'asile came too late in France, and it is possible that in the fury of revolution all these excellent institutions have been swept away.* We, perhaps, have yet time enough before us to bring such a plan to maturity, and reap the benefit, and I shall now proceed to show from the experience of what has been done, how much might be expected from such a movement on a large scale.

---

* Since the above was written, the author has had the satisfaction of learning from an acquaintance who has lately visited Paris, that the Salles d'asile are still in active operation, as well as another charity in which infants are received and nursed during the absence of the mother at her work. A certain sum is paid weekly by the mother who carries her infant early in the morning to the *Crèche*, as it is called, which consists of a large room where cradles, nurses, &c. are provided: the child is washed and nursed, and the mother returns twice in the day to give it the breast, or if weaned, it is fed by the nurses, and a certain degree of education is begun even here, which is continued in the *Salle d'asile*. There are several of these *Crèches* in Paris, under the superintending care of the ladies of that city, who seem to have found in these, and similar institutions, a more satisfactory employment than in the ordinary dissipation of women of fashion. May our English ladies walk in their steps thus far at least!—Nov. 1850.

CHAPTER II.

The Origin and Purpose of Ragged Schools.

SOME few years since, there might have been seen in St. Mary-street, in the town of Portsmouth, a poor shoemaker, who, while sitting on his stool, and working diligently at his trade, was surrounded by a group of ragged children, whom he was instructing. His name was John Pounds, the son of a sawyer employed in the dock-yard, and of course poor. An accident which he met with when about fifteen years old, increased the difficulty of earning a livelihood, but this did not dishearten him; he worked on at the trade he had taken to, and not only maintained himself, but was able to adopt and bring up a nephew, who was, like himself, a cripple.

It was in thinking over the best mode of educating this boy, that the thought struck him, that the companionship of another child would render learning easier and pleasanter to him than if he had to study alone; he accordingly found a companion for his nephew in the son of a poor woman, his neighbour. The experiment was successful; so successful, that in a short time two or three others were added to the class. But even when the boy, for whose sake he first became a teacher, no longer stood in need of his instructions, the good shoemaker did not abandon the class he had thus formed; on the contrary, he added to its numbers, until it consisted of upwards of forty scholars, including twelve little girls. The pupils he taught were the destitute and neglected, "the little blackguards," as he called them, and many a time he has been known to go out upon the public quay, and tempt such as these by the offer of a roasted potato, or some such simple thing, to enter his school. There is something in the voice and manner of an earnest, truthful man, which is irresistible; it is an appeal made to that divine image of which there is some trace still left in the most corrupted heart; and it was seldom, therefore, that the summons of John Pounds passed unheeded: and when once at the school, his scholars seldom needed urging to come a second time; for their master taught them not only "book-learning," as he called it, but his trade; if they were hungry, he gave them food; if ragged, he clothed them as best he could ; and, added to all this, he joined in their sports. What wonder that they loved him, or that when he died,* and his death was sudden, at the age of seventy-two, the poor children, who then formed his class, wept, and some of them fainted on hearing the news.

No very long interval elapsed between the death of John Pounds, and the introduction into Aberdeen of a Ragged School, upon a much larger scale. The ceaseless action and reaction of ignorance, idleness, and misery upon crime, seems to have struck Sheriff Watson, as it had already struck the Portsmouth shoemaker; a society was formed to supply the means of affording instruction to all the vagrant children of the city, and the plan was carried into execution with partial success. Still something was felt to be wanting, and it was at length suggested that in addition to the education given to the children, they should be supplied with food and industrial occupation. Great was the outcry with which this proposition was at first received. " What? do you mean to treat thus all the young beggars in Aberdeen? Who ever heard of such a thing?" But the question was answered by the opening

---

* In 1839.

of the school upon this footing in October, 1841. A few friends favourable to the scheme had advanced £100, and they began with twenty scholars, and by March in the next year, the numbers had mounted to sixty.

This good beginning was followed up after a time on a larger scale, and the police were instructed by the magistrates to convey every child found begging in the streets, to a large room which also served as a soup kitchen; and thither on the 19th of May 1845, seventy-five children, boys and girls were taken. The scene which ensued was almost indescribable:—confusion, uproar, quarrelling, fighting, and language of the most horrible kind, were to be encountered and vanquished. The task was a hard one,* but the committee before the even-

---

* " It was fitting " to use Sheriff Watson's own words, " that such a meeting should be constituted by an appeal to our Universal Parent, and the messenger of the Gospel prayed that He would send down His light and His truth to enlighten and direct; that He who had said ' suffer little children to come unto me,' would of these little ones make children of the kingdom of heaven; that the Father of the fatherless, and the God of the needy, and of those who had none to help them, would adopt them into His family, and make them joint heirs with Christ. The language and the accent of prayer have

ing succeeded in establishing something like order. The children were then told that this place was open for them to return to daily, and they were invited for the morrow, but were at the same time told that whether they did so or not, they would no longer be allowed to beg, since food no less than instruction was offered to them there. The next day the greater portion returned; funds flowed in for the support of the undertaking; the working classes took a lively interest in it, and whilst the wealthier inhabitants of Aberdeen contributed during the year about £150 towards carrying it on, the working classes subscribed no less than £250. The report of the committee of managers states as the most gratifying result of this happy combination of all classes for each other's welfare, " that whereas a few years since there were 320

---

always a soothing and softening effect, and these rude Arabs of the city, who would have resisted oppression however severe, and authority however legitimate, were subdued by the earnest appeal to the Fountain of mercy on their behalf; their hands which had hitherto kept hold of each other, fell down by their sides; their eyes which had been suspiciously directed to the opposite party, were turned towards the ground; and they gradually assumed the attitude of humility and devotion."

children in the town, and 328 in the county of Aberdeen who, impelled by their own or their parents' necessities to cater for their immediate wants, prowled about the streets, and roved far and wide through the country, cheating and stealing their daily avocation, — now a begging child is rarely to be seen, and *juvenile crime* is comparatively unknown."

The example being set, it was ere long followed up by other benevolent individuals, and in 1844 a society, under the title of The Ragged School Union, was formed for the purpose of forwarding the good work, and assisting with pecuniary aid where the funds were inadequate.*

---

* The first impulse to this movement in London was probably given by a Society formed as long ago as 1750, under the title of " the Society for Promoting Religious Knowledge among the Poor." Its constitution was similar to that of the City Mission (founded in 1835) and Ragged School Union, one rule being " That the members shall be selected from Christians of various denominations." Porteus, bishop of London, Romaine, John Newton, Thornton, Wilberforce, Rowland Hill, were among the names of those who joined this society. From this sprang the London Missionary Society, the Religious Tract Society, the Bible Society, and the London Sunday School Society, and it was among the Sunday School Society Teachers and City Missionaries that the plan of Ragged Schools was mainly matured.

Unfortunately, the very circumstance which made these schools most desirable, excited a prejudice against them, and checked the current of charitable liberality. 'Thieves and vagabonds were here received, kindly treated, and instructed; they had thus a better chance than the children of honest labourers, whom no one sought out;—it was offering a premium to vice.' Many very worthy people insisted that 'misery is the appointed punishment of sin, and that to attempt to rescue these children from the state into which their own and their parents' misdeeds had brought them, was detrimental to society by confounding the distinctions of right and wrong, lessening the divinely appointed penalty of crime, and thus weakening the deterring

---

The first school so *designated* appears to have been that in Field Lane, but several isolated schools on that principle had been set going at different times, both in London and elsewhere, long before the term *Ragged Schools* was adopted. Among these the name of Mrs. Fletcher ought to be mentioned, who gathered out of the streets at Laytonstone thirty or forty poor houseless, neglected children, taught and fed them; and of Mr. Thomas Cranfield, who died in 1838, who had hired a room, and opened a Ragged School. Mr. Robert Stacey first conferred with Lord Ashley on the subject in 1844, and assisted in forming the Ragged School Union.

force of such examples of suffering.' Others again insisted 'that the evil habits in these children would be too strong for any instruction to eradicate, and that the attempt was a mere throwing away of time and money which might be better employed.' Nay, it has even been urged that the congregating together at these schools led to greater corruption, and that the incentives to crime were likely to be increased by bringing so many young thieves and vagabonds together. From these various reasons, the funds of the Ragged School Union have been so curtailed, never amounting to more than £520 yearly subscriptions,* that it is wonderful that so much, rather than so little has been done.†

---

* The donations have been much larger, but these do not form a *fund*.

† Whilst writing the above, a newspaper announcement was put into my hands which I gladly transcribe here. May the example be largely followed:—"The foundation-stone of the Holloway Ragged Schools was laid on Wednesday by Henry Pownall, Esq., chairman of the Middlesex magistrates. The interesting ceremony was attended by a large number of visitors:" also " a splendid building has just been completed in Newport-street, Lambeth-walk, for the education of the ragged children of the vicinity. The entire building, inclu-

As things stand at present therefore, it **can** only be regarded as an experiment **on** rather **a** large scale, to ascertain how far certain principles are practically applicable; and **as** this experiment has now been carried on for a sufficient time to show how the system is likely to work, the promoters of it have a right to claim a hearing. It will therefore be our business to examine whether they have made out their case, and whether, supposing they do so, it **may** have been in consequence of accidental circumstances, or whether they have gone straight to those great motives of human conduct which when once put in action will always lead to such results. Perhaps the best way of condensing this inquiry within due bounds, will be to take the history of one of these schools, where the writer can vouch for the details from personal knowledge.* The following is the simple narrative of one of the teachers at the B— street school. " Mr. — tells me you wish to know something of the

---

ding the out offices, workshops, masters' residences, &c. covers an area of 3000 feet. It has been erected by the munificence of Mr. H. Beaufoy, the eminent distiller of Lambeth, at a cost of £3000.

* Names are not given for obvious reasons, but by application to the publisher, the locality of the school here referred to may be learned.

origin of our school. I was invited on the first of October, 1843, (i. e. to assist in establishing a school of the kind) by the city missionary. It appears that the missionary had given out that this school was to be opened on the Sunday for boys who had no shoes or clothes to go to other schools. About six or seven of us met in the little room in B— street, on the Sunday afternoon, little expecting what we should have to contend with. We opened our school this first Sunday afternoon, with about twenty lads from twelve to twenty years of age: their object, as I afterwards found, was to have a lark We attempted to teach them, but they immediately wished to leave the school; this we opposed: the boys got resolute, so did some of the teachers. This very soon broke out into open rebellion, and had the teachers been *all* as resolute as some were, we should all have had our heads broken. Some of the teachers used great violence, and when the boys saw the blood flowing from one of the boys, in consequence of one of the teachers holding him so tight by the neck, I could see and hear that they were urging one another to the attack. I stood a calm spectator, but I at once saw the necessity of breaking up the conspiracy, by diverting their minds to a new object, and holding out a prospect of some reward to those who were not so forward in the rebellion; and thus we managed to divide them. We soon got several of the bigger boys on our side, and such a scene followed as I shall never forget: some swearing, some dancing, some whistling, and the teachers looking some of them as pale as death, and some quite exhausted: and thus we got over our first afternoon. Some of the teachers I have never seen since: most of the boys were reformed.

"Some short time after this, one Sunday evening, I was left to manage the school with one little timid man, when about seventy boys came in, and literally crammed the place: and seeing no physical force capable of resisting them, they at once put out the lights, and attempted to carry off every thing worth a penny, in the place; such as the candlesticks, books, boys' caps, &c. I at once authorized some of the bigger boys, whom I knew something of, to defend the rights and property of the school. I set four of the best and stoutest round the book desk, which they defended like men; others I got to help me to clear the room and get lights, &c. and I found myself at last with sixteen who all took part more or less in restoring order, and who begged of me to let them stay to the prayer meeting which we used to hold every Sunday night* after the school; and it was a sight to see these sixteen boys on their knees before God, listening silently to the prayers that were offered up to God for the salvation of their rebel companions, who had caused so much confusion. Not that these sixteen were so much better than the rest, for they were nearly all of the same sort, but the fact is, that you may always divide the interests of a mob of poor people, if you know how to go to work."

A more inauspicious beginning can hardly be imagined: we shall now see the working of this school in one of the worst neighbourhoods in London.† I shall again select from the simple

---

* This worthy man was a Wesleyan.

† When we opened our Ragged School in B— Street, I was told by a policeman that he never was on duty in such a depraved neighbourhood before in his life. He had been on duty in Westminster, Saffron Hill, St. Giles, and he would defy any one of those neighbourhoods to produce a more abandoned set of thieves than there was in that neighbourhood. He said he knew about a hundred of them. A policeman said he knew from his own experience that the Ragged School had done more good to the boys than anything else had done before. He knew the C— family: the reformation in all that family

journals of the worthy man who so bravely stood the burst of the rough outset of the school.

"The beneficial effect was felt in the neighbourhood almost immediately after its establishment, by the shutting up of two notorious houses; one a coffee-shop named by the boys themselves the Dark Den, where they used to share the produce of their plunder, the other a house of ill-fame,* kept by the mother of one of the boys. The son and daughter of this woman we took into our school, and they were the means of breaking up this den of infamy. The son, about nineteen years of age, has been seen reading the Bible to them; and the girl has been led to see her own and her mother's wickedness,† and by a stern opposition to their for-

---

was astonishing." C — was the third admitted into the Industrial School.

* This house is now used as the Industrial School.

† This girl went into service, and the following letter from the master, a respectable tradesman, to one of the teachers of the school, will show that the reform so far, had been lasting.

"Dear Sir.—I am sorry to state that owing to Ann C— having such violent pains in her head, she is obliged to leave us and go to the Hospital. Her sister has filled her place with us. No fault to find with either of them.
Yours truly, H. W—.

mer habits, succeeded in breaking up the establishment. One of the lads' mothers told me that she considered her son lost, and she should have reason, as long as she lived, to bless the friends of the school. I was told by another mother, who had three lads in the school, that her children now were not like the same: they were so kind and affectionate."

The school had been carried on at first by tradesmen who, out of their small means, gave both money and money's worth, namely their time, to this charitable work; but they were not long without assistance. I again quote the journal. "On the 24th of January, 1847, a gentleman who had long indulged the hope that he should one day have the opportunity of testing the Christian principles that he professed, arrived. On the day above stated, the poorest of the poor, and an agent who had cherished the same hope, met together," and if ever we may believe a special blessing from on High was extended to human endeavours, it was so here.

It was very soon perceived that the extreme poverty of many of these children rendered theft or mendicancy their necessary subsistence: they had not learned to work at any lucrative employment, and if they got a few pence to-day by holding a horse or sweeping a crossing, they were again destitute on the morrow. Many of them had no place to sleep, and passed the night under arches or doorways. At last the plan which had been adopted at Aberdeen with so much success, was thought of, and by the help of increasing patronage, set on foot. The teacher from whose journals I have quoted, was a shoemaker, and he undertook to instruct three of the boys in his trade. These boys were supplied with food and lodging, as well as instruction in the trade.

" Two or three boys were in an indescribable state of destitution. Their father dead, deserted by their mother, and no friends but the teachers of the Ragged School,* who previously to their

---

* The following autobiography was written by one of these boys at the request of the teacher:

" Sir,—I will give you a short account of our lives from 1843 to 1848. Sir, I went to Liverpool with my father, and my father died there, I was there for some months. They gave me eighteen pence, and told me to go home again, and when I came home I was in great distress. I slept about in cabs and shutter boxes, and a many times in the street, till I gave myself up as lost. One day I went to Mr. — [the teacher] to tell him I was going to the workhouse, when he told me he had

coming into the Industrial School set them up in the lucifer match trade. We have known boys to buy their stock of lucifer matches the last thing on the Saturday night, and go without food all the day on Sunday that they might secure food for every day the next week.

The industrial class was commenced on the 17th May, 1848, with the two G's and J. C. This last "had for some time past been known as a notorious pickpocket and petty thief; having been brought up under very disadvantageous circumstances. His mother was a drunkard of the vilest character and a pest to the neighbourhood. C— had been repeatedly imprisoned, and when taken into the class had neither shirt, shoe nor stocking, and the rags that hung on him

---

spoken to a gentleman about me, and he was a friend to me; and my brother was not given to thieving, nor had any wish for it, and I hope we never shall. We are very thankful that we are where we are, for we have seen a plenty for our age. We have been very kindly treated by many gentlemen. All things work together for good to all that love God. We mean to try and love God. S. G. aged nineteen. G. G. aged twelve."

The elder brother after learning the trade in the Industrial School, is now with a shoe-maker: the younger is apprenticed to Mr. —, one of the benevolent teachers of the B— Street School. Both lads have conducted themselves perfectly well.

were filthy. He was one of the mob who endeavoured to destroy the public peace in Trafalgar Square in March, 1848. He stated that he was tired of the life he was then leading, and begged hard of his teacher that he might be put into some better means of obtaining an honest livelihood."*

The conduct of these boys fully justified the selection; they were cleanly, orderly, and in all respects perfectly honest, and so sensible of the advantage they had derived from their in-

---

* "Last January (1847) at one of our schools, it was determined that prizes should be given to the deserving. They were so badly off, that it was conceived best that the prizes should consist of fifteen pairs of boots. I was in the chair at the distribution. The schoolmaster told me that these boots would not all be given to the most deserving, because it so happened that some of these were not the most destitute; and some of these boys, of their own free will, went and requested that the boots might not be given to them, but to others who were in greater want. Now here was an instance of self-denial that it would be difficult to match in any other class of society; these boys, accustomed only to live for themselves, now entering into the length and breadth of the apostolic precept, 'Look not every man on his own things, but every man also on the things of others,' I would invite you to go and ascertain, by personal experience, the evil, and the mode and manner of the remedy; and it is for you to determine whether these efforts shall

struction, that J. C. hearing there was a design of enlarging the class, went to the Teacher and said that he was anxious that two of his old associates should be admitted, that they might be saved from ruin. He, and the other two, offered to divide their three rations into five, and thus share their food with those for whom they were anxious to obtain the same advantages. They were reminded by the teacher that in this case they would go hungry themselves. " We do not mind that, sir," was the answer, " we are used to it;" and the arrangement was made as they desired, nor ever after repined at. Since that time the industrial class has been enlarged to fourteen; no instance of dishonesty in regard to the goods necessarily placed in their hands has occurred, and C—, now respectably married, was for some time one of the superintendents of a portion of the boys. His strict honesty was

---

fail, or whether they shall be multiplied. I cannot express too much affection for those excellent persons with whom I am here associated. Their zeal, their perseverance, and that, mark you, carried on in obscurity, where their efforts are only known to God and their own hearts, —these seek from you a hearty co-operation."

Speech of Lord Ashley, delivered at the Annual Meeting of the Ragged School Union Society, June, 1847.

tested very sufficiently by an accident; for on carrying home some of the work the boys had done, he was paid by mistake a sovereign instead of a shilling;—before he got home he discovered it, and, returning immediately to the house he had just left, gave back the money. The same sort of results may be seen in the reports of the different ragged schools in London and elsewhere; affording on the whole a strong presumption that juvenile profligacy is generally cousequent upon the misconduct of the parents; and that few, if the advantages of a regular industrious life were offered them, would be slow to embrace them.* " Five years' experience in Ragged and Industrial Schools," says the teacher already so often mentioned, " has most fully convinced me that the human family is one, and that the difference of character which exists, is the effect of circumstances. At least two thousand children have passed through our Ragged

---

* I may perhaps here be allowed to repeat a singular anecdote, although it has already been published. A notorious thief asked to be allowed to go over one of the Ragged Schools in London, and then said, " I shall subscribe a sovereign annually, for if these schools had been in existence some years ago, I should not have been what I now am."

School since its commencement: I have watched and questioned many of them, and have invariably found that the cause of their distress and misery may be traced to the parents, more especially the mothers. We have taken some of the most destitute out of this Ragged School, and have had as great a diversity of character, temper, and organization, as it is possible to conceive. We have had those lawless creatures who have been chained, whipped, confined in the black hole, and subjected to every species of punishment without effect. Some of them have told me that they never intended to stop when they came to the school . . . . . . I have made myself thoroughly acquainted with all their secrets, and there is, I believe, the greatest confidence between us: they are all convinced that I would make any sacrifice to make them happy, and all they study is to know my will, and that is their law. There are only one or two gentlemen who can stoop low enough to reach these poor ignorant wretches. I am a great advocate for the cultivation of the intellect, but let our English legislators, school-masters, and Christian ministers, combine with their laws and theories, the exhibition of a Christian character, and live and act as the author of Christianity did."

"One great difficulty is to get agents to carry out the work: we cannot hire, nor buy faith . . . . . If you get the affections, the work is nearly done, and you may mould them as you please. Supply them with the necessaries of life, a bed to lie on, water to cleanse themselves, a fire, and a clean place to sit down in, good conversation, and interesting books; and then, as surely as spring succeeds winter, and harvest follows seed time, so surely will you see the moral wilderness become a fruitful garden. We have seen it, and we do see it."

Of the few gentlemen who "can stoop low enough," for these wretched creatures, one is known to the writer, and to his kindness, seconding with a longer purse and a higher kind of education, the benevolent efforts of the first teachers, much of the success of the school is owing. He has on various occasions taken a class of the ragged children to his house,* has got his friends to give them experimental lectures on such points of physical science as were within their comprehension, and has awakened in them thus a love of intellectual amusements which will not easily sleep again. After an evening of

---

* There were about twenty-five of them.

this kind, concluded with a song or two, and some conjuring tricks, one of which produced slices of gingerbread for the happy party, one of the boys was heard to exclaim, " This beats all the gaffs !"

Reader, have you ever entered a Ragged School? If you have not, suppose yourself at my elbow, and make a visit to B— Street. You pass through rather a dirty street, and enter then a very dirty alley, near the lower end of which you see a door, and, on entering, find yourself in a clean and comfortable apartment, where from sixty to seventy boys and girls of the most squalid appearance, are assembled in small groups, round several well dressed persons. They are reading or spelling, or perhaps tracing letters or words on their slates. You see among them a sharp eager look, which tells of wits sharpened by necessity: you speak to one; you receive none of the usual homage paid by poverty to riches, but you receive the appellation of " teacher," which is in their mind the noblest they can give; and in a moment, without the least disguise or *mauvaise honte,* the child will tell you his history, and talk as freely as to an old friend. The gentleman above mentioned, enters; the children are immediately anxious to take his hat, and place a seat for him; hang about him with expressions of affection, and seem to consider him as their own. Presently the reading ceases, a gentleman mounts a kind of rostrum, a little elevated above the children, and addresses them. He explains the moral doctrines of Christianity, exhorts them to follow the example of our One Great Master, who was himself poor and suffering;* encourages them to hope in His goodness, and to see in the present zealous endeavours to ameliorate their condition, a proof that His mercy indeed watches over them. Many of the children listen with the most fixed attention; you see that at any rate they understand what has been said; sometimes a general " Thank you" marks their satisfaction when the lecture is concluded; and often shrewd remarks shew that they have fully apprehended its purport.†   A prayer and a hymn sung by

---

* " I have suffered more than ever Jesus Christ did," said one boy to another, " he was never three days and three nights without food as I have been." " Yes but he was tho'," said the other, " he was once forty days and nights without *grub*."

† " I remember hearing one of the boys at the Ragged School say, on leaving the school one evening, " Good night, teacher; I hope we shall meet in heaven." " I hope we shall, my lad," was the answer. On another

the teachers and such of the children as are capable, concludes the meeting; and whilst the singing is still going on, the teachers gather and dismiss small lots of nine or ten at a time, so as to ensure their quiet departure.

Such is the mechanism of a Ragged School; but without the warm benevolence which animates the teachers, and which shows itself in all their actions, little would be done.* When the writer was present in the B— Street School, a wretched ragged child appeared at the door— two of the teachers instantly went to meet him with the kindest of greetings, took him by the hand, led him to a seat, and arranged all for his comfort; he was shirtless and dirty, but sharp and intelligent, and his quiet orderly conduct showed that the aspect of the place had had its

---

occasion I heard one boy remark to another that he "got nothing by coming to school." "Why you gets the word of God," said his companion, "do you call that nothing?" (Private Journal).

* A man then a notorious thief, said to one of the Missionaries who attended him in prison, "I always considered religion all humbug, and the parsons humbugs, who were paid for praying and preaching, but when I see people taking young thieves who are following in my steps, out of the streets to save them from ruin, this is something like Christianity."

influence. He had felt that he was no longer wholly forsaken, and probably another being was here in the course of being rescued from misery and ruin.

It is from these miserable outcasts of society that the so-called dangerous classes are recruited, these swell the numbers of juvenile offenders,* and puzzle legislators and rulers as to the means of disposing of them. Have not these truly Christian teachers solved the problem, and shown

---

* In Mr, E—'s Journal I find the mention of one lad of so desperate a character, that even his former companion C— despaired of him. "After six months' training on our system of mercy and patience," continues Mr. E—, "he is now in a good place, paying as far as he can the few shillings he borrowed of Mr. ——— He comes to my house every night, and tells me all his tales whether good or bad. I have watched him and tried him, and I find that right principles are planted, and will grow and bear fruit if cultivated. He had been in prison several times, and flogged." By his own statement it appeared that "he had been one of the luckiest thieves in London." His mother stated to Mr. E—, who is in the habit of visiting the homes of his scholars, "that there was a time when her son was so unkind and wicked, that it was a grief to her to see him; but it is now a comfort to be where he is. He reads to his father; especially the third Chapter of John, on the necessity of being born again. Six months ago he hardly knew his alphabet."

that if any class be dangerous it is because we by our neglect have made it so, and that if, instead of building prisons and paying jailors, we could find persons who believed in the Christian doctrine enough to act upon it, one quarter of the money spent in these expensive establishments would render two-thirds of them useless, by preventing crime instead of punishing it?*

The gentlemen engaged in this good work, and by whose agency so many of their fellow creatures are rescued from so miserable a fate, give up but a small portion of that time which most persons without regular employment feel to hang heavy. If instead of yawning or sleeping over a newspaper in a Club-house, the idlers there were to go forth only a few hundred yards;—for misery and luxury are in close juxta-position in London,—they might find occupation

---

* One or two of the boys who had attended the B— Street School went one evening into a Chartist meeting in the neighbourhood, and compared what they heard with the doctrines taught at the Ragged School. On one of the speakers denying or doubting the existence of a God, one of these boys exclaimed, "Then who made the sun?" They were ordered to be turned out of the place by the Chartists.

which would be more patriotic than swelling the numbers in a division on a political question, for on the success of this movement probably much of the prosperity of England depends:—more exciting than the Derby day, although the affairs of the nation be second in importance to it—for they are the souls of men which are running the race·—and producing more real satisfaction, and winning more real affection than perhaps such idlers ever attained to before.

Had a few more of the numbers of our legislature known more intimately the working of these schools, we should not have seen the just hopes of the teachers disappointed by the refusal of the small national grant which enabled them to send out to the Colonies such of these lads as had proved themselves trust-worthy. Surely it is a poor legislation which requires crime to qualify for colonization, and which prefers the expensive machinery of policemen to take, judges to try, and prisons to receive the convicts previous to their transportation, to the simple plan of reforming the children who would otherwise be criminals, and then allowing them a free passage to colonies which dread the being flooded every year with fresh cargoes of vice, but who would gladly receive an orderly set of workmen and servants.* " I have a letter from a friend lately arrived from Australia," says Lord

---

* The following are extracts from some of the letters sent home by the boys and girls who went out the year that the Government bestowed a grant to pay their passage. It is impossible to read them without regretting bitterly the short-sighted policy which has refused a continuance of this grant.

"April 29th. 1849. Port Adelaide, S. Australia. MY DEAR FATHER AND MOTHER.—I write to you in good health and spirits, hoping that this will find you quite well. I am very comfortable indeed. I have got a very nice comfortable situation as servant of all work. I have £16 per year. I think I shall do very well if I behave myself. I have got into a family that is very religious * * * All that you have got to do is to behave yourself, and conduct yourself with propriety. * * * It was the captain that got me this place, for he said he would not leave us till he saw us all in good Places * * * Give my kind love to Emma, and tell her I wish she was here * * *

Your affectionate daughter, CAROLINE WALKER."

The writer of the following left England in the "Marian" with twelve other emigrants in October, 1848. He had been partially taught shoe-making prior to his leaving.

" March 11th, 1849. DEAR BROTHER.—I hope this note will find you well and hearty, the same as it leaves me. I wish you were here with me to share what I have. I am getting from thirty to thirty-six shillings per week, and paying twelve

Ashley in a late speech on the subject, "speaking very highly of the conduct of our emigrants.

---

shillings for board, lodging, and washing. I hope Jane will come out. I have sent word to Mr. Vanderkiste to send her. Girls are more wanted than men. I would advise you to come if you can. The dogs live better here than men do at home. It is now Sunday night, and I am going out for a walk round the houses, and have got a pound note in my pocket if I want it. * *

I remain, your affectionate brother,

JOSEPH FREDERICK JAMES."

The next letter was written by a youth who left England in the "Lebanon" for Port Phillip, in October, 1848.

"Port Phillip, New South Wales,

DEAR FATHER AND MOTHER, SISTERS AND BROTHERS.—This comes with my love, hoping to find you all in good health as it leaves me at present. * * * The country is a beautiful place, and I have got a good master. I get ten shillings per week, and board and lodging for the first six months; after that, I shall get I dare say, double, as I am at present a shepherd. * * I go out of a morning at sun-rise, and all I have to do is to see that my flock don't part. I lie down and read all day, then at sun-set I come home, have my supper, and go to bed. Coming from England to Australia is like coming from a dirty town to the Garden of Paradise. You can get fine beef or mutton $\frac{3}{4}d$, $1d$, and $1\frac{1}{2}d$, per pound. The young girls have at the rate of £28 per year. * * * If you would come out, I should never think of coming home * * * shoe-makers and tailors, if they are steady, soon make a fortune in this country, &c.

CHARLES PHILLIPS."

I am assured by many who know Australia well, that none make better shepherds than hand-loom weavers of Spitalfields, for, going out unbiassed by any system, they readily adopt the

---

"Port Phillip. May 8th, 1849.

I am with a very good master. I am now getting my food and £12 per year. It is a most delightful country, plenty of work, and plenty of every thing. I wish you would come; men's wages at a farm house from £20 to £25 per year, and rations. I am getting on first rate. Tell my school-fellows . . . the best thing they can do is to come here. W. Chester."

"Port Phillip. May 8th, 1849.

. . . I am keeping sheep at one of the out-stations, for £12 per year, but expect soon to get £15. It is a very nice country for those who like to make their minds happy and comfortable, as very few do except us Bushmen. Alfred Bickerton."

"Gulong, Port Phillip. May 19th, 1849.

We did not stop at any port till we arrived at Port Phillip . . . Masters came on board to hire us. We agreed for what wages we thought proper. I engaged with a master who cannot read or write, to keep his accounts, for wages at the rate of £24 per year, with board, washing, and lodging. * * * I will not come home for nine or ten years at the least; and by being steady, in that time I could save a little fortune.
John Connell."

We entered the Bay of Port Phillip, and staid there till the Monday following, when the settlers

system most simple in use, and easily fall into the required position. As to hanging about towns, out of 220 sent out, all have obtained

---

came on board to hire us. I got myself hired the first day, at £5 per year, and my victuals.
WILLIAM WIGGETTS."

The following is the closing paragraph on a most interesting and well written diary of the voyage, bearing date from December 21, 1848, to April 4th, 1849:

"THUS after a pleasant voyage of nearly four months, I have got a situation with W. Salter and J. Barnett in the Bush, about 100 miles up the Campaspie river. We have £16 per year, with all our food, and a hut to live in.
J. N. MARTIN."

Port Adelaide. June 23d, 1849.

RESPECTED SIR,—I have the happiness to inform you of the realization of my own, and I believe no less of your anxious wish, of arriving at Adelaide. Every thing has transpired to our comfort that we could desire, but I am sorry to put a cloud on the sunshine that we have experienced, in saying that rumour, with her hundred tongues, has run through the vessel, reporting that we Ragged School lads are bad characters; but those who said it, when confronted, denied having used any such expressions. * * * Wishing all the gentlemen connected with the School happiness on earth and hereafter, I beg to subscribe myself, together with my companions, who join in my good wishes,
J. REWER. W. HOLMES. W. PYNE."

Addressed to a Member of the Committee of the Hopkins Street Ragged School, Golden Square.

employment at good wages, and in most cases found their way into the Bush, so that the difficulty does not really affect us, and with regard to Sydney, it has been made a stipulation on the payment of all monies (whether government or otherwise) over which I have had any controul, that it should not be applied to emigration in that quarter. It is an overgrown town, and boys sent there would be very likely to return to their old haunts, and we should only be transplanting them from one scene of vice to another. In only two instances have complaints been made as to the conduct of our emigrants, and that was on board ship, which was entirely repressed in less than a fortnight; much of the statement put forward was a gross exaggeration. Considering the numbers sent out, and the characters we had to deal with, I think the reports received a complete triumph; but this imposes an additional responsibility; for, seeing what may be done, we must go into "the highways and compel them to come in." *

The expense would not be more than half that now incurred: statists might be satisfied

---

* Vide "Report of the Annual Meeting of the Grotto Passage Ragged and Industrial School." June 26th, 1850.

with that—but if there be any who *really* believe what they profess to do—what must *they* feel of satisfaction in the prospect of promoting the temporal welfare of the country, by contributing to the happiness here and for ever of a large number of her most miserable progeny!

CHAPTER III.

Why are Ragged Schools successful?

THE details of the last Chapter can hardly leave any doubt as to the fact, that the benefit derived from these schools have been both great and lasting. No accidental whim could influence so many human beings of different dispositions, breeding, and locality, during several years; and we must come to the conclusion that some great spring of human nature has been touched, which had not been reached before, at least not in this age. Once, only once before, within strictly historical times, have we seen an influence exerted as powerful and effectual: it was when Christ, and his immediate successors in the work, preached holiness and brotherly love to the world, and rich and poor abandoned all factitious distinctions, and met before God as equals. The slaves of Greece and Rome were as profligate as, and more brutalized, for the most part, than, the so-named "Dangerous Classes" of modern Europe, but from among them was selected many a martyr, whose constancy the persecutors thought to overcome the more readily because of his degraded condition; courage being considered as the privilege of freedom. The ennobling tendency of Christianity disappointed their calculations, and slave and master frequently shared one fate, as they had shared one baptism.

The warmth of Christian feeling cooled as abstruser dogmata were brought forward: the heart is little influenced by what puzzles the comprehension; and when the belief of abstract doctrines began to be considered as essential to salvation, the understanding was too frequently so busied with their definition, that the simple rules of the early Christian teachers were neglected. With controversy came uncharitableness, and very soon, from loving, the Christians changed to hating one another. The ruling sect under the plea of caring for the salvation of the ignorant, punished all who attempted to preach any doctrine but the one established by edict; and every fresh sect made it more difficult to unite the family of Christ into anything like fellowship. "Listen to us," says one party, "we have the keys of heaven, and can give you free entrance there. All those who do not enter with us will most probably perish everlastingly."

The denunciations are retaliated: the Dissenter asserts that the clergy of the Establishment do not preach the Gospel: the clergyman marks with severe reprobation all schismatics and heretics: a simple man listens to one and the other, and finds so little that is attractive in either, that he probably remains in a state of indifference, and sleeps while these uncivil epithets are bandied to and fro; saying, perhaps as a naval officer once told the writer, " It is not my business to understand these theological points. I look to my own affairs, and they must settle theirs."

Was it then to found a theological faculty that Christ taught and died? Was it to set apart an ecclesiastical body zealous for abstract dogmata? Surely not. It was to the poor and the needy, the weary and heavy-laden, that the good tidings were to be announced: what had they to do with abstruse discussions as to the mode in which grace is communicated? It was enough for them that they asked and received it; that courage came with the occasion, and that the heart felt the proffered peace. Holiness before a God of purer eyes than to behold iniquity; brotherly affection to all, integrity, and a strict fulfilment of all domestic duties; these were the characteristics of a Christian; and many an one who had never heard of abstruser doctrines, lived and died happily by following the simple rule of "Do unto others as ye would they should do unto you," and imitating the example of their meek and holy Master. Alas! how many can we suppose would be saved, if a strictly logical definition of all the doctrines of one church or sect were requisite to the process? And if any can be saved without this, why not all? The scholar may exercise his ingenuity; that, to many, is a pleasant occupation: but let him be content to leave to the simple-minded the simple precepts of the first preachers of the Gospel.

Such would be the reasoning of a conscientious man approaching the subject without any previons prejudice; but the best have the prejudices of education, at least, hanging about them; for what has been taught us as essential, is not easily thrown aside, even though our better reason should be convinced that it ought to be so; and I will not undertake to say, that the worthy persons who have so cordially united in the work of the Ragged Schools, have entirely discarded theirs; but here accident has done what perhaps reason would not have effected so easily; for persons of all sects having seen at once the desirableness of the work, saw also the difficulty of it if any sectarian differences were allowed to be put forward. They loved the souls of these children better than their own opinion on a few disputed points; and, by a kind of tacit agreement, Wesleyans, Baptists, Independents, &c., joined with members of the Established Church, both high and low, in the room in B— Street, to teach the fundamental doctrines of Christianity without touching at all on more difficult tenets; and the children saw that Christianity was indeed an all-embracing system, since those who parted in their places of worship, met in their charities,—acted by the same rules,— won love by the same kindness.*

Nor is it to the children alone that this really accidental circumstance has been useful. To the teachers themselves, thus compelled to make the distinction as to what part of the doctrines currently taught among persons of their persuasion,

---

* A teacher in one of the Ragged Schools had been severe in his conduct to several of the children: one of them took an opportunity to ask another of the teachers "if Mr. —— was a Christian?" "Yes, doubtless." "And will he go to heaven?" "I trust so." "Oh then, I don't want to go to heaven, for I should not like to be where he is." Let those who think religion can be *enforced* remember this.

is really essential to salvation, it has been of great service, by opening their minds to more enlarged views, and showing how possible it is to be true servants of Christ, notwithstanding differences of phrase, or even contrariety of opinion upon what they have now been compelled to feel, are non-essentials. The Churchman, the Independent, the Wesleyan, the Baptist, who have met in fellowship to teach the same Gospel to the poor and destitute, can hardly hereafter stand aloof from each other, as aliens from the household of Christ. They must feel that they are servants of the same Master, though acting in different capacities, and all, from their natural imperfection, falling short in some way, of perfect service, though striving to the best of their judgment and knowledge. " Who art thou that judgest another's servant? to his own master he standeth or falleth; yea, he shall be holden up, for God is able to make them stand."

The deepest feeling, generally, in the minds of the very destitute is, a sense of the contrast between their own state, and that of the affluent whose luxury strikes them at every turn. They complain of the supremacy of the few, by means of which they have monopolized the good things of this world, leaving only labour and want for the masses: and the natural consequence of this is, an antagonism between different ranks which destroys all Christian brotherhood between them. The greater the destitution, the bitterer is this feeling, till all kindly sympathy is lost, and a sharp enmity takes its place. These miserable and neglected wretches revenge themselves on society by preying upon it, and feel the sort of pride in a course of successful robbery, which a wild Indian would do in a good hunting expedition: the danger does but give zest to the sport, while success procures abundance for the time being.

When the duties of honesty and morality are preached to such as these, if drily taught, a suspicion naturally arises that self-interest is the motive of the preacher: robbery is an evil, and prosecution is expensive, and if men could be persuaded not to steal it would save the instructor's money and goods. It is very difficult to avoid making this impression when attempting to win attention to the lessons of religion; and, till this is removed, all our attempts to improve the heart will be futile. Probably it was this feeling which produced the scenes described at the opening of most of the Ragged Schools; but the teachers here calculated, and calculated wisely, on one great instinct in every human breast: i. e. the weary longing for kindness from our fellow men, and the delight of finding it. These unhappy children had seldom known what it was, even from their parents : those who were not orphans, were many of them the children of thieves, or persons of that description, had early been trained to bring their small pilferings to the common stock, and were beaten if they returned empty handed. Perhaps in this the parent calculated ill, for a practice enforced by blows is never a favourite one; and the thief is no more made to love his profession by flogging, than a schoolboy is made to love his studies by the same process. They enter a room where persons, at least in easy circumstances, are found voluntarily to expose themselves to insult and ill-usage, and to respond only by gentle expostulations. These persons say to them " We have been taught by our Master, who was himself poor, to love all his brethren : we compassionate you, we wish to better your condition; will you yourselves join in the effort?" The first feeling is perhaps incredulity, but the next is confidence in, and affection towards those who seem to have no earthly interest in what they are doing.

"If a man love not his brother whom he hath seen, how shall he love God whom he hath not seen?" is the acute observation of the Apostle John: and it is only by awakening human affection for human virtues that the unenlightened are led to higher spirituality.* A hard unbelief in any Divine superintendence is the common state of mind among these children: they have never heard, they have never thought of it; and if they are told of a Father in heaven, they attach so little that is pleasant or loveable to that name that it is rather repulsive than otherwise: nothing therefore is available in such a case but the mere human instinct. Higher and holier thoughts may come hereafter; but, in the first instance, the teacher must be loved: nay, so necessary was it to accommodate the weakness of human faculties, and the strength of human instinct, that the last, best message of God to man was spoken through the lips of a man whom

---

* "I say Mr. E——" said one of the B— street boys in speaking of Mr. —— (the gentleman already mentioned) "I should think he is better than God. He is too good for heaven." The next step in this boy's mind would be that heaven consists in the being always with such persons; and then comes the hope of future bliss as the first rude incentive to spiritual thought.

we might both love and imitate; and most of the earlier converts to his doctrine were more moved by the " gracious words" of the Teacher, than the intrinsic excellence of the precept.

It is not easy for those who have never seen it, to form any conception of the fond affection with which these children regard their favourite teachers. In the B—— street school, the girls put together their little savings in order to buy materials for the working a pair of slippers, and other trifles, for the gentleman teacher from whom they had all experienced so much kindness; and they brought the work, when finished, to the lady superintendent to present. Mr. —— offered to pay for it, but this they declined; he then asked the cost of the materials, that he might at least defray the expense; but this they refused to tell, and he was at last compelled to receive their present, in order not to mortify them.

The sharpness of observation and promptitude which a life of thievery makes necessary, has the effect of developing the intellect at a very early age; and thus the bane carries its own antidote; for these uninstructed lads receive knowledge much more rapidly than the less excited brains of the children of steady parents will allow them to do. The B—— street school too has had an accidental advantage; for Mr. ——, the teacher to whose especial exertions a large share of its success is owing, having himself at one time doubted the truth of Christianity, and satisfied his own mind by rational argument; he has been able and willing to answer questions on this head, which, perhaps many who have received what is called a more enlarged education would scarce trust themselves to grapple with. And here we come upon another great law of our nature; for the moment that a farther development of its powers is begun, the intellect claims its part, and those that were at first satisfied with the mere instinct of love, now feel that the understanding must be convinced ere they can be quite at peace. It was this which in a very short time led the first Christians to engage with so much vehemence in controversies relative to the nature of God, the mode in which he was present in Christ, &c. It is a necessary phase of progress, and cannot be avoided but by that dead sleep of the intellectual part which would leave man a mere gregarious animal.

We may now sum up the causes of success shortly as follows.

1. The preaching the gospel in its simplicity,

unincumbered with abstract dogmata; the very form in which the apostles and first teachers of Christianity presented it to the uninstructed multitude.*

2. The exemplification in the manners of the teachers, of that law of love; thus winning the hearts of their scholars, and showing that what they teach to others they themselves believe also.

3. The satisfying the intellect, as fast as it developes itself, no less than the instinctive affections; and thus engaging the *whole* man in the right course.

Had a philosopher been set to discover the best mode of influencing man, he could have devised no better plan: for, in the uninstructed, as in children, the natural instincts are strong, but the intellectual faculties weak: both therefore must be guided by instinct till reason gains strength. The social affections and the love of imitation are among the strongest of instincts, as we see in the animal world no less than among the human race: and thus the wish to please, and to resemble those we love, are the

---

* That "we should love one another, even as God hath loved us." "The pure in heart shall see God," &c.

first motives to well-doing among such. As the higher faculties gain strength from the cultivation begun by the aid of the affections, they require something more; and then we must be ready to "give A REASON for the hope that is in us;" and carry the mind forward to objects which have awakened curiosity, with the reverent, yet free inquiry which alone can bring conviction, because it alone can elicit truth.

To him who has believed on the mere ipse dixit of a beloved parent, or a favourite teacher, the time will come when he will say to himself, " Mahommedans, Jews, Pagans, all believe they are right because they have been so taught by their parents and spiritual guides: — I have no more cause *to know* that I am right than they have;"—and when this thought arises, if the *proof* be not ready, the intellect overpowers the affections, and, however painful the wrench, he discards the belief which cannot be demonstrated: or if that require too great an effort of courage, sinks into indifference, satisfying the eyes of men with outward forms, in which his understanding prevents his heart from any longer taking a share.

Half the evils of our time have resulted from not duly understanding these laws of human nature; and, with the best intentions in the world, many of our religious teachers have nearly extinguished religion among us, by forcing dogmata on children, and the uninstructed poor, who are in the condition of children, and need therefore to be led by their natural instincts and affections; and then requiring unreasoning submission and obedience from persons whose minds have been awakened by long intellectual culture. The first turn away from the cisterns which hold no water to comfort and refresh them, with parched lips and weary hearts—what are dry dogmata to them? they understand nothing of these things — the second shrink from anything like thraldom of the intellect; too readily consider the call for unreasoning faith, a proof that the system will not stand the test of argument; and fall into the state of the philosophic heathen of the higher orders, who thought it good policy to support the state religion for the sake of the people, but considered it as not worth their own thought. Were the plan reversed—were the poor and the ignorant taught as Christ taught them, by moral apologues and short precepts, by ministering affectionately to their wants, and feeding them as babes, with the milk of the word, we should hardly now be complaining of danger from the lower orders: and had those whose intellectual culture made them long to fix their religious hopes on the basis of sound argument, been encouraged " to prove all things, and hold fast that which is good," many a corruption of the pure doctrine of Christ, many a superstition, and many a prejudice, which now are stumbling blocks in the way of the man of science, would have been long ago removed.

The teachers of the Ragged Schools have found true philosophy without looking for it :— let us not despise it now that it is found ; but having learned the secret of their success, use it " for the glory of God and the improvement of man's estate"— and make England an example as to how the " Dangerous Classes" may be dealt with, so as to make them the strength, not the weakness of the country.

The inefficiency of ceremonial and dogmatic religion is still more felt where Romanism is the established form of Christianity; and has been fully recognised by those French writers who have treated on the means of reforming those unfortunate classes whose perversion was a source of so much danger to the community. "One of the causes," says M. Frégier,* "which has the most weakened the effect of Catholicism on the masses, and yet more on men of cultivated understandings, is the multiplicity of required practices, and the length of the offices. The almoners, or rather the prelates who direct them, will not deviate from the received traditions: this is orthodox, no doubt, but it is not charitable,—it is not Christian. The sentiment of religion is a sympathetic affection, like all other affections which give a great impulse to the mind; and like all moral instincts, it is needful in order to awaken it at first, as well as to afford it full development, that we should accommodate our teaching to the wants of those who are to receive it, modified as these will be by the age, the sex, the condition of the person. Hence these women† have always received with gratitude the religious consolations brought them by charitable ladies; women themselves, who could comprehend their first weakness, and the circumstances by which they have been led away; while they

---

* Des Classes Dangereuses de la Population, tom. 2, p. 254.
† The prostitutes in the prison of St. Lazare.

have always shown a dislike to the nuns, who, taking their stand on another world than this which we inhabit, wish to subject them to observances which fatigue without amending them, or even offering them any alleviation of their misfortunes. Hence it is that they are cold and unmoved while attending mass, and receiving the instructions of the almoner, while they experience great pleasure in singing hymns written in their own language, and which they can understand. All those who have observed our prisons are struck by the wrong method pursued by the chaplains, and are grieved at the irremediable mischief which they are involuntarily doing to the cause of religion."

This must always be the case where a ceremonial religion takes the place of that of the heart and understanding, and if it be thus hurtful in excess, it becomes a matter of concern to all conscientious Christians to take care that religion shall never become a system of wearisome observances in their hands. It is the tendency of all establishments; and since of late the public mind has taken a bend towards ceremony, and the building and ornamenting of churches has sometimes been more considered than the cultivating the minds of those who are to fill them, it is well to see what the result is in regard to the spiritual welfare of those who are subjected to its yoke. The attending public worship may be an act of homage to the Giver of all good, which the soul delights to pay to the Father whom in its inmost recesses it loves and honours; but it may be also an act of cold conformity, utterly without influence on the life of the man, and valueless in the sight of God; and if prolonged to the point of creating weariness it invariably becomes so. He who forbade long prayers and observances calculated to catch the eyes of man, knew human nature well; and in proportion as we disregard his merciful directions, and insist on abundance of outward forms, and " vain repetitions," we weaken the feeling of religion, and throw obstacles in the way of our own salvation.

CHAPTER IV.

Amusements.

I HAVE left this subject for separate consideration because it has hitherto been very little noticed, and because it is in itself highly important. Every physiologist knows that the human frame is incapable of continued exertion: sleep and rest must recruit the exhausted muscles ere the strain can be resumed. The brain, too, is a bodily organ, and that also must have its hours of rest, or permanent disorder will be produced, and the faculties and the health will suffer serious injury: but among the heathen at the period when the apostles preached, the recreations were of a nature so degrading, for the most part, to the moral sense, that we find the whole system most unsparingly denounced, and the singing of hymns appears to have been the only amusement which the first Christians permitted themselves. Indeed, whilst the mind is enthusiastically excited in the pursuit of any great object, recreation is not wanted—sufficient

ring incidents of a life so employed, afford the requisite change of occupation; thus the teachers of the new faith, travelling from place to place, continually occupied with the converts already made, or those they hoped to make, felt no weary sameness in their lives. They held in their hands the destiny of the world:—and how many bright anticipations of unknown good to come must have warmed their hearts and filled their thoughts to the exclusion of all other things! How vain must all the common amusements of life have seemed to these men! How disgusting the coarse or frivolous pastimes of the multitude!

The same observation may be made to a certain extent with regard to all founders of religions orders, or leaders of sects: THEY want no other amusements than those which the active carrying out of a great project affords them: their enthusiasm fills them with dreams of results scarcely less important than those which filled the hopes of the apostles, and they scorn all lesser pleasures. But these active minded men forget that their disciples cannot have their feelings,—that the mind of him who learns and of him who originates thought are, if not fundamentally different, at least in such a different stage of development, that they require a different treatment. They forget that when all the arrangements are ready made, the doctrine laid down, and the machinery complete, their followers will have none of the occupations which have filled their own time and thoughts, and left no room for other recreation. A series of dry observances takes the place of a life of active exertion and spirit-stirring incident; and if the founder have, like most founders of sects, endeavoured to enforce a total renunciation of the lighter enjoyments of life, many of his followers, finding the yoke too heavy to be borne, throw it off, and rush into immoral dissipation; others carry it unwillingly while the heart is far away; the sect gradually loses its vitality, and two or three generations later, it becomes the mere lifeless corpse of its former self.

It was the peculiar excellence of Christ's teaching and example, that he called for no such renunciation: he mixed in society; shrunk not from the feasts of his countrymen when invited; and forbade his disciples to wear a mortified appearance, or to practice extraordinary austerities: but the later converts to Christianity were unable to appreciate the divine wisdom of this middle way, and an utter renunciation of earthly things was more and more enforced. This had all the usual consequences: many relapsed into heathen observances for the sake of the diversion, and we find the writings of the third century already complaining of the improprieties consequent on frequenting marriage feasts, theatrical exhibitions, &c.—an evil which might have been avoided had they endeavoured rather to supply innocent amusements, than to proscribe what the human frame so imperiously demands. On the other hand, persons of more tender conscience and stronger will, finding the temptation too great as long as they mixed in the haunts of men, in order to guard against what they cousidered their own frailty, withdrew from secular life altogether, and thus began the religious orders, and the troops of hermits, inhabitants of the tops of pillars, &c. who forgetting the rational precepts of their Master, seemed determined to turn again to the weak and beggarly elements from which he came to rescue them: and instead of seeking to imitate Christ, who " went about doing good," seemed to have taken for a model some Indian Gymnosophist, and to have thought to serve God by disabling themselves from doing any good at all. Derangement of intellect very generally followed the total seclusion of a life in the desert, and many of the hermits of the Thebais grew wild and savage as the beasts who were their sole companions. The religious orders, on the contrary, living in communities, but without the complicated interests of domestic life to keep the mind awake, soon sank into indolence and sensuality: repeated prayers as a daily tax upon their patience, and narrowed their minds to the small interests of their convent.

Later, we find among the reformed churches the same mistake made: those who wished to attain superior holiness, proscribed the gaieties of life as though they had been sins; and whilst the enthusiasm of a new movement lasted, they succeeded in impressing their own views on numbers, who, when this first fire burnt out, found the system wearisome; and though shame prevented them from abandoning it altogether, kept to the letter without the spirit. The society of Friends, Wesleyans, &c. &c. who have all in turn proscribed amusements, have all found in the lessening numbers or diminished zeal of their members, that something is wanting in the system: and, if they would be honest, would confess that, as in the case of a mechanist who has omitted to allow for the force of friction, their machine must work itself to a standstill. They have wished to be more holy than their Lord commanded, and they have ended by becoming less so, because, unlike Him, they have not known " whereof we are made," and without that knowledge it is not easy to promote the well-being of our fellow creatures.

He who would lead man to right doing and its consequent happiness, must look long and deeply into his own bosom ere he begins his attempt—and not only must he seek a knowledge of human nature there, where he can study it most at his leisure; but he must endeavour to know and enter into the feelings of the class no less than of the individual which he has to deal with. Ignorance on these points has been the fruitful source of many evils which in the minds of a large number have brought the whole system of Christianity into disrepute. Had those who resorted to persecution by way of enforcing a belief which they considered necessary to salvation, looked into their own minds—had they asked themselves if any amount of torture would alter their own habits of thought so as to make them in the innermost recesses of the heart embrace an opinion which they believed to be erroneous,—would they have hoped to torment people into a salutary belief? Outward profession they might attain, but what is outward profession in the eye of God? We can only believe from proof, or from obstinate prejudice which in its overweening confidence will not listen to demonstration: but the persecutor offers no proof, and the prejudices of his victim's mind are against him; all he attains therefore is at best a slavish submission, and if the heretic's belief endangered his soul before, it will surely endanger it yet more, when a hypocritical conformity caused by base fear is superadded to whatever else there may be of wrong.

Another panacea against error has been propounded in our days, and submission to the Church* has been called for, as being of power to controul wrong opinion, and consequently to make better Christians; but he who submits his mind to the dicta of another, has in fact no opinion at all; for we cannot alter our conception

---

* This is the phrase, but it is not a proper one: for submission to the Church in the sense now given to it, means submission to certain men appointed to office in the Church. The Church itself—Ecclesia, is nothing less than the whole body of believers.

of the truth to suit that of another mind. Every man has as individual a mind as he has a body, and can no more fashion it to the similitude of his spiritual pastor, than he can bring his eyes to be of the same colour. Submission then, is indifference; and this is sufficiently shown in countries where Romanism prevails. Indifference in the higher, and superstition among the lower orders, take the place of any thing like vital Christianity. If we attempt to rouse enthusiasm, like all passionate movements which depend on bodily emotions, it cools down again into rationality; and if we attempt to controul enquiry, we do but pave the way to utter unbelief. Thus we return to the point that if we would really do good among our fellow creatures, we must accurately study their nature.

Few have chosen to acknowledge to themselves that a knowledge of physiology is almost essential to the spiritual teacher; and yet whilst the animal body is, by the will of the Creator, so closely united with the spirit, that they mutually influence each other very largely; it can hardly be maintained with any show of reason that he who would mind the human race, can wholly ignore one half of human nature. He who would avoid temptation, or teach others to avoid it, ought to know whence it is likely to arise, as well as the best means of escaping it; but this knowledge is not to be found in theological books; and if such subjects are ever touched upon in such, as in some ancient books of casuistry they are, the style in which they are treated, makes the discussion not merely useless, but hurtful. Let us clear our way by considering what temptation means, for we rarely arrive at any satisfactory conclusion without a correct definition of terms.

Temptation then, is a craving of our nature for some indulgence which is either not then to be allowed, because other circumstances forbid it, or which being in excess requires to be curbed. Thus a man who has been in the habit of recurring to the stimulus of strong liquors whenever he feels exhausted, at last becomes so habituated to it, that he experiences an uneasy sensation if he has it not. The temptation then is strong, but it requires to be met, not by fasting, which but increases the bodily need, and consequently makes the temptation stronger, but by amusement which shall occupy the mind agreeably and innocently, and lead to the forgetting the importunity of the animal temptation; or if this do not suffice, by drugs which shall for a time supply the requisite stimulus, and thus lessen the temptation to transgress. The man who is in earnest in his wish to amend, might thus be taught by a wise friend how to strengthen his resolution, or rather (what is equivalent to it) how to make the temptation manageable.

All temptations arise from the animal nature, for unless the emotion were strong and involuntary it would be no temptation at all; and our animal nature has strong instincts given it for its preservation, good in themselves if not allowed to exceed the proper bounds, bad if carried to excess. It is not therefore by prayer against the excesses which our nature is prone to, which of necessity leads us to dwell mentally on what is already becoming too frequent and exciting a thought, that we shall vanquish it. A prayer for judgment; for a blessing on our right endeavours, is purifying and sustaining to the mind;—a prayer against particular temptations is but an indolent endeavour to cast on another the toil we shrink from ourselves, and should be thus characterized. Reason was not given us for nothing; and I believe few would succumb to temptation, who would take rational methods for lessening the bodily impulse, and diverting the mind from dwelling upon it. Hence the great importance of providing innocent recreation for the mind and body, and of making both frequent enough to prevent the uneasy craving from being felt, which might lead to excess. The rest of the seventh day has provided a constantly recurring day of repose which puts aside all temptation to idleness; for it comes often enough for refreshment:—were not this appointed, continued toil would seem like a duty to those who depend on the labour of their hands for a maintenance; and the man who felt exhausted and took a day for repose, would be blamed as a sluggard, perhaps consider himself so, and think that as he had done one wrong thing under a temptation which mastered him, he was already so far gone, that another fault or two would not much alter the account. By legitimatizing the degree of repose requisite to the human frame, it has been made to assume a sanctifying instead of a degrading influence.

Again, had marriage not been appointed, thus hallowing the relation between the sexes, and making it the source of all that is most amiable in human nature, the natural tendency of the race must have been indulged, for it is a propensity implanted by the Creator; but it would have deteriorated instead of ennobling mankind: as indeed it does in every case where the marriage tie is disregarded. Let us not fight against God then, by endeavouring to eradicate any natural bent, but let us sanctify it, as the Apostle recommends, by doing " all to the glory of God."

The demand of the human mind for recreation ought to be thus legitimatized, and only regulated as to quality and quantity. There is scarcely any other human want which has not been cared for by the law, and its rational and moderate enjoyment legalized: in the matter of recreation alone, an unjust distinction is made between the poor and the rich; and whilst these last, who least need such aids, can at all times procure amusements of at least an innocent, and often of an elevating tendency, the poor have nothing left them but the low public house. Places of assemblage for dancing, music, or theatrical diversions, are either put down as nuisances, or are so uncared for, and left in such bad hands, that they ought to be so: yet it would be very possible to make these things conducive to good morals, and to use them as means to civilize and raise the mental standard of the population. Something man must have to recruit him after labour*—the mere eating and going to bed after a day's work, will not fill up all his wants, and the want of the mind, if not so readily appreciated at first, is in the long run even more severely felt than that of the body: the question then is solely—shall this want be so satisfied as to raise or to degrade? It is vain to ignore the need: it is a part of our nature: the only question is as to the mode of supplying it.

This becomes an especially anxious care where we would effect the voluntary reform of persons

---

* We have heard of a ship where the plan of allowing the men rational amusement was tried with great success. In wild countries the men were taken away for several days by the captain on hunting and fishing expeditions. The result was, they returned to their work with redoubled vigour—the indulgence acted as a reward to the good men, and stimulated the ill-disposed to obtain a good character. It was remarked how little punishment there was in the ship alluded to; the fact was that the forbidding the idle or ill-disposed to partake in indulgences was a very severe punishment, *but a mode of punishment impossible where no indulgences are granted.*

" One of the difficult points to overcome with British seamen is their passion for drink, but to allow them rational amusement much tends to improve their tastes and habits."—*Letters on the Navy.*

hitherto very little accustomed to self-controul. To fix minds, till then never exercised in application, on any study, or any consecutive thought, for more than a very short time, would be impossible—the brain, till strengthened by use, is incapable of long protracted attention, and for such persons, as for very young children, the teaching by amusement becomes a necessity. Learning to read, to write, and to cast accounts are wearying to the attention, and it is found by the teachers of Ragged Schools, that even though there is generally a good will to learn, the attention of the pupils very quickly flags, and can scarcely be kept up for above half an hour at a time. In common schools the master forces on the unwilling scholar by the aid of punishment, but in schools where the attendance is wholly voluntary on the part of the children, to punish would be to drive them from you. Here therefore an accidental circumstance has again led to the acknowledgment of a great truth; namely that the usual system of school castigation is a mistake, and that if we wish our pupils to improve, we must suit the length and nature of their lessons to their mental state, taking care at all times never to press learning on so as to induce weariness, and by pauses, and good humoured conversation with them, to make the period of study pleasant. Nothing is a more general taste than that of music, and in the B— Street School it has been found very advantageous to set songs of an innocent or moral description to known and easy tunes, which the boys could learn and sing for their own entertainment and that of their companions,* besides the hymns taught them. Two or three concerts of this kind, in which the boys and teachers were the sole performers, have been held, and with the greatest success; some bread and butter or pudding concluding the entertainment to the satisfaction of all.

This is as it should be: the *enjoyment* of right doing should be sensibly felt to strengthen

---

* At the time when all the world was mad after Hullah's plan of teaching vocal music, a class of this kind was established at a small country town near some friends of the writer. One night having strolled within reach of a little hedge ale-house, they saw four labouring men come and seat themselves on the bench. They immediately began a glee which they sang very tolerably, and after spending about an hour in this way, they rose and departed, having had one pot of beer between them. How great an improvement was this on the usual style of visits to public houses! Unfortunately the Hullah class was discontinued.

the young resolution, and as vocal music is the most attractive, as well as unattended with any expense, it presents itself at once as one of the easiest and best modes of supplying the great desideratum of innocent amusement. The slight knowledge of the science which is requisite to singing in parts might be communicated with ease: the nature of a third, fifth, and octave, is easily understood, and the very exercise of thus forming the common chord by means of different voices, is amusing: the ear once formed to these intervals would very soon become acquainted with the others, and the few chords which enter into ordinary compositions would be easily acquired. The knowledge of music thus given would not be great, but these are the first steps of music as a science; and if any among the children thus taught the rudiments, should choose in after years to go further, he has at any rate a foundation laid for instrumental no less than vocal performance.

The great fault of the usual teaching in schools is that it is altogether empirical, and therefore tiresome; were the first steps of all knowledge made rational, and therefore interesting to the scholar, we should generally find less disinclination to learning of any kind; for the mind would be occupied, and might find subjects for after thought in the explanations given. It is so difficult to break through long established habits, that had not the Ragged School system been a thing entirely *sui generis,* the great problem as to how instruction can be made most available, would probably never have been so fairly put and solved; and even now there is danger that former habits and prejudices may sometimes tempt very worthy persons into thinking that a greater degree of severity would be both more effectual and more godly. I think I have proved from the constitution of man's nature that it is not likely to be more effectual; a few words more may be said as to its godliness.

There is an idea very prevalent that the path of duty is a rugged and a painful one, and those who tread it are led to expect that their reward is to be wholly in another state of being, and that here they must embrace suffering as their portion. We can hardly imagine that a WISE GOD wishing to induce his creatures to arrive at that future happiness, would allow the difficulties in the way of it to be so great, that few would have physical courage to surmount them; still less can we suppose that a GOOD GOD would thus narrow the numbers so fearfully, of those who should attain to blessedness: and when we find any of the notions which we have received, appear to contradict the known nature of God, it is a sufficient reason for revising them. Christ has said that his yoke was easy and his burthen light; we can hardly, in the face of that declaration, suppose that the Christian religion proscribes the comforts and pleasures of life. It then becomes our duty to consider whether the path of duty be so rugged as it is represented; and whether, if we can smooth it in any way, we are not working the will of God by thus making his paths strait and easy to walk in. When we pray daily that His will shall be done on earth as it is in heaven, if there be sense in words, it means that it shall be willingly, lovingly, and cheerfully done;—that the doing it shall be pleasure; the having done it, happiness. Let us then remember the nature it has been His pleasure to give us; a mixture of the animal and the spiritual:—the emotions belonging to the animal, the enduring will to the spiritual; and we shall see that in order to bring the *whole* man to God, we must interest the pleasurable emotions in the business as well as the will. The first will be awakened by kindness, the second influenced by rational convietion. But the emotions are naturally transitory, and however a wretched child may be led to abandon his evil ways at first by kindness, if he have no rational expectation that a better course will bring him real enjoyment, when the personal influence ceases, the inducement to well doing ceases also. It becomes important then to point out God's promise, that if we will seek spiritual good, all the rest shall be added; to show that the path of duty is also the path of happiness; and by giving a foretaste of greater enjoyment, to show that there is something worth striving for. It is upon this plan that the teachers of the B— Street School have proceeded, and their complete success is such as, from the principles above laid down, was to be expected.

Although I have mentioned music as one of the amusements which almost all are alive to, there are others for which a taste might be awakened of a no less ennobling nature. Drawing especially is a thing in which many children find pleasure, and which also by means of a black board and chalk may be practised at very small expense. The accuracy of eye which even a slight knowledge of this art engenders, is essentially useful in every sort of mechanical operation. A few large prints hung on the walls and a board or two properly prepared would be all that would be required to enable many of the children to amuse themselves pleasantly in the school when weary of other things, and would open to them not only a source of recreation but of after profit, should they arrive at enough proficiency to be pattern drawers. The reading to them sometimes of an amusing story, or travels, by some one who can give it point and effect, would create a higher taste, for the reader could stop to explain what was difficult, and the cheap literature of the day supplies enough of really good publications to meet the demand of the poorest, if the taste for such could be aroused. All these and many more modes of recreation are possible, not only in Ragged Schools, but in those parochial ones in which the children now only try how little they can learn during four or five years of forced attendance, and were this matter attended to, we should in a very few years see a very different population growing up. Our scientific and industrial advancement has proceeded and is proceeding at an accelerated ratio;—are our people to be the only raw material which is to be subjected to no better system of treatment than it was in the days of our fathers? Already we have everywhere machinery and contrivances which no ordinary servant or workman is able to manage properly—we complain of the stupidity of the lower orders, but should we not rather complain of our own?—We set brute matter to work, and forget that it requires intellect to guide it. The steam engine is applied to all kinds of purposes,—electricity is made our servant,—but the human mind, that finest of all machines, the most powerful of all forces, is disregarded, and we think we have done all if we have *fed* the poor! Let us hope that the dawn of a better time is before us.

CHAPTER V.

Conclusion.

I HAVE now fulfilled my promise, and examined the grounds of the success which has attended the teachers of Ragged Schools; and if I have shewn, as I think will be allowed, that these lie deep in human nature itself, we shall do well to make use of the experience thus gained. If we examine the statistics of crime, we shall find that for one wilful criminal,—by wilful I mean one who has by his education and station no previous training to vice,—there are nearly a hundred who are offenders against the laws because no one has cherished in them the feeling of that higher moral law, which is the foundation of all society. They have been educated in the way they should *not* go, and when they are old they do not depart from it.

It is a great mistake to suppose that because reading, writing, and other usual school knowledge has been withheld, that therefore no education has been given. The mind of the child must receive its bent from the circumstances by which he is surrounded, and the companions among whom he is thrown, and this is education. By these and not by the merely mechanical attainments above mentioned, the character is formed.

It is not therefore by the almost universal diffusion of the power to read and write, that vice is to be curbed, or virtue strengthened: these are but means that may be used to good purpose, but which may also be used for the contrary, and it seems astonishing that when the necessity for the farther instruction of the lower orders has been so generally recognized, it should not have occurred to the promoters of what is called education, that the mere power of pronouncing sounds, or expressing them by letters, gives no impulse to mental progress, and thus a child may pass through a national school, and come out reading fluently, writing a good hand, and able to repeat by rote some few questions on doctrinal points, without having gained one idea; without having formed any habit but that of marching steadily round the schoolroom; without having developed even the germ of a spiritual existence; animal he entered, and animal he leaves it, and then, if hunger presses, or indulgence is coveted, what hinders him from unscrupulously seeking the gratification of his animal needs? There is a possibility indeed, that with the power of reading a taste for less gross pleasures *may* be kindled; but this in the ordinary course of things is left entirely to chance: nothing is done by the school towards awakening it. The master, for the most part, is not capacitated by his education to give instruction of a higher order; the clergyman examines the children in the Church Catechism and other catechisms of a like kind, where the answers if not learnt by rote at first, become so by frequent repetition, and rarely pauses to inquire how much they understand of the words they thus repeat.* Who then educates these children? Not the schoolmaster, not the clergyman, for they understand not what they say, —but the poverty, the discontent, the possible squalor, drunkenness, and violence of their

---

* In the course of a catechizing in church, the writer once heard a clergyman ask a child what he meant by the grace of God? "*Trinity in unity*" was the answer! Why had this doctrine ever been taught the child in such hard words? He could have fulfilled all his Christian duties equally well had he never heard of them. How much he understood the answer shows.

homes. These awaken thought, for they cause suffering, and it is the awakened thought which forms the character.

It is an ungracious task to strip away the covering from specious delusions: it is so pleasant to sit down satisfied that all is as it should be, that few are willing to forgive the person who rouses them from so agreeable a dream; but if it be a dream likely to end in a frightful reality, it is a piece of moral cowardice to shrink from doing an act of duty because it may offend. It is in this spirit, and not with any desire needlessly to carp at the honest though misjudging efforts of a large number of my countrymen, that I animadvert on the mistake made in regard to the instruction of the people. The machinery is sufficient, the good intention undeniable, why then do we find so large a proportion of criminal prosecutions? If real education were given it would not be so. But *real education is not given.** Nothing, or next to no-

---

* The following questions are culled at random from an examination by a master sent from the London National Schools, to ascertain the state of proficiency of a country school.

" How did the Apostles compose the creed? Were they all together, or did each compose a part?" A

thing, is done to counteract the evil influences of the world: the children are not taught what the dangers are which lie around them, nor the reason why they are dangers. They hear from loose companions of pleasant sins: no one tells them that these so-called pleasant vices are but the first steps towards crime, poverty, and disease: no one attempts to open their minds by such general instruction as shall rouse the intellect, and make them capable of finding pleasure in innocent and ennobling amusements, and when religion is spoken of, it is as of a hard and weary service here, only to be compensated

---

dead silence followed, for the children, as it happened, had learnt more of their duty than of theology.

"Who was St. Athanasius?" Another dead silence.

"In what light does the Catechism consider Baptism in the first part?" "As a sacrament." "No, that is in the second part," was the reproof of the examiner. Of course no other rational answer could be given, but the children were condemned as so incorrigibly stupid that it was useless to examine them further.

Was this a proper style of examination for boys destined to be agricultural labourers, little farmers, and tradesmen? The first question must lead to a false conclusion,—the next was utterly useless,—the third, which might have been made instructive, seemed like a trap. If this be the manner of conducting an examination, what is the school instruction likely to be?

by an hereafter which offers nothing desirable to one whose mind rises very little, if at all, above the beasts which aid him in his labours. Whilst the school teaching bestowed on the children of the poor is such, it is not wonderful that a country lad, if he fall into the company of town bred vagabonds, should at once yield to their seductions, and help to increase the numbers of the Dangerous Classes.

Christianity was not given as a system of dogmata to be learned by rote, and we have now seen that all its best fruits can be attained without teaching any of those sectarian differences of opinion which have so split the church of Christ, and sown disunion and uncharitableness where there should be love and peace. Why then should they ever be brought forward as matters of importance? If the precept "do unto others as ye would they should do unto you," were properly commented on, and made the rule by which all actions should be squared, it would be of far more use than all the catechisms usually taught, which load the memory without conveying any idea to the mind, and which from being wearisome, are remembered only as an irksome task, which will be at an end when they leave the school.

If we would have a moral population we must civilize and give a taste for higher pleasures. Savages are always grossly vicious, and wherever the animal nature engrosses the largest share of attention it must be so: for man has faculties of a higher order, and if these be made subservient only to the gratification of bodily propensities, the man is curtailed of his due proportions; the faculties dwindle, and the animal part itself suffers from the wants which his mental powers are insufficient to provide for. The lesson which Ireland has given ought to have convinced us by this time, of the danger of leaving any part of the population in a state of semi-barbarism.

Were the method of teaching better, the time given up to it is sufficient for a much larger share of instruction than is now attained; but the system is bad from the beginning: the parents have no idea of training their children but by blows, and the pulpit, which might be the vehicle of useful instruction on this head, is too often devoted to moral and religious admonitions of so trite a nature, that the thousandth repetition of them cannot now rouse the attention of the hearers. Constituted as the human mind is, any subject, however interesting, becomes wearisome by frequent repetition; yet the clergy persist in repeating what may be good *per se*, but which is not good for the people if they have heard it till they are tired of it. Were there not an almost cowardly dread of doing anything not exactly customary, the Sunday instruction from the pulpit might be made available to a thousand useful purposes, but most especially to that most useful of all, the teaching parents how to manage their young children. They might be told how children should be dealt with by them as we ourselves are by God. He makes our sins our own scourge, and inflicts nothing arbitrarily :—so should it be in the education of children,—they should be allowed to suffer the consequences of wrong doing; but blows are no necessary consequence of any action of theirs, and therefore give no moral lesson. If a child tells a lie, to disbelieve him afterwards when he is anxious that his assertion should be credited, is a proper punishment; a flogging has no connection with it, and cannot be inflicted when the boy grows up; he knows and depends on this, and punishments of this kind have therefore no permanent moral effect. The distinction between the animal and the spiritual nature might be made clear, and parents might be instructed in like manner, from the pulpit, as to how they may avail themselves of this in the guidance of their families: the lives of good men might be given as holy lessons: the history of the progress of Christianity, of the temporal as well as spiritual benefits it has conferred,—in short, a course of instruction no less useful than amusing might be given,—if the language were made studiously plain,—which would do much towards amending the state of the lower orders.

Turn where we will, we find that what we complain of as an evil is but a result, and that to remove it we must go to the cause; as, for instance, if you find the children in the National schools in the country districts heavy and dull in learning, it is because during their first years the mind has never been roused to thought in any way; the parent who has no concern beyond his daily food, teaches his child nothing else—the bounded interests of a country village awaken no wish for more knowledge, a little gossip respecting his neighbours fills up the time not employed in solitary labour; the public house offers the animal luxury of stimulating liquor, and no higher or deeper thought is ever awakened. Is the child who goes from such a home likely to profit much from the school instruction, after the intellect has been in a dead sleep for seven or eight years?—those precious years, during which the brain is acquiring its full growth, and consequently the faculties are taking the bent which they will preserve through life.

There are only two ways of meeting this difficulty—by mending the parents, and thus rendering the first impressions of the child more favourable to mental development, or, if the parents cannot be mended, by receiving the children at an earlier age—and here Infant Schools may be made of infinite use, by giving a capability for future thought; by awakening curiosity, and shewing that amusement and learning are compatible. Probably establishments on the footing of the *salles d'asile* in Paris might be organized in most *towns* in England with good effect; but in the country young children cannot be sent a mile or two from their home, and the only chance there, is by the better instruction of the parents. The example of King's Somborne and some other places, shows what *might* be done in this way; but till the clergy can be persuaded generally to adapt their instruction better to the capacity and situation of their hearers, little amendment is likely to be effected: for who is ever influenced by what he does not understand? Nay, even though the preaching be intelligible, if the attention of the hearers be called rather to the abstruser doctrine than the practical part of Christianity, the spirit of the Gospel is crushed under hard, dry discussions which have little or no influence on the life, and are therefore of minor importance. It should be remembered too, that human language being originally formed only for tangible objects, is in its very nature incapable of an exact definition of spiritual things; and probably no two minds will ever come to exactly the same notion of what is utterly intangible. It would be wiser and more charitable to avoid, as far as possible, such subjects as "minister strife," and trusting that God, who "knows our infirmities," will pardon involuntary errors of this kind, leave each individual to shape his opinions into the form most conducive to his own spiritual progress. Let us in the mean time, like St. Paul, be content to "know Jesus Christ and Him crucified," as our example and guide,—endeavour to win men to wear His easy yoke and "follow after the things which make for peace,

CONCLUSION. 125

and things wherewith one may edify another." *

We have lately seen the Church of England distracted upon the question of the colour of a vestment :—was this worth the breach of charity which it created? and did it matter whether the message of God to man was delivered by a person in a black or a white dress? If the message was a true one, the clothing of the messenger was surely a matter of no import. A fresh cause of dissension has now arisen on the subject of baptismal grace; but who can settle this question? " The wind bloweth where it listeth, and thou hearest the sound thereof, but canst not tell whence it cometh or whither it goeth; so is every one that is born of the spirit." † If we see no good works, we have no proof of this spirit-birth, for again we are told " by their fruits ye shall know them," and whatever grace may have been accorded is withdrawn if we " grieve the Holy Spirit" by our wilful wrong doing. What concern then have we with anything more than the ascertaining by a careful examination of our life and motives, whether we

---

* Romans xiv. 19.   † John iii. 8.

are bearing the fruits of the spirit? to decide how we arrive at this point is a mere matter of curiosity. Such would have been the decision of a follower of Christ, from his Master's own words. On the other hand, if we argue the point philosophically, we must assuredly conclude, that the Deity having made man capable of intellectual, or in other words, of spiritual happiness, it can only be by cultivating this intellectual part that such happiness can be attained; and that no ceremony, or course of ceremonies, can make a gross nature spiritual, or make intellectual enjoyments acceptable to one who loves nothing but the animal and transitory pleasures of earth.

If we would lead men to Christ, we must practice no less than teach His precepts; for what person of common sense can suppose that we believe things which we never do, to be absolutely necessary to our happiness;—or on the other hand, that our ordinary and daily life is such as must bring on us irremediable misery. Will not an untaught, but rational man say, "I am convinced that fire burns, and therefore I never put my hand into it—you tell me that none but the meek and the holy can be happy, but you are neither meek nor holy:—whatever you may tell me therefore, it is clear that you do not believe it yourself." This conclusion is frequently drawn :—the writer in talking with the poor has been told—" Yes, this sounds well, and no doubt if it were so, things would be better than they are, but nobody else thinks thus," and the ill effects of this practical lesson of unbelief, meet us at every turn.

It is worse than useless to dispute over points of no practical import, while the land is fast relapsing into an absolutely pagan ignorance. Who that loves the souls of men can turn from the great question of how they are to be made partakers of a happy immortality, to the position of an altar; or the form of a pulpit, or the compliance with an obsolete rubric, at best but an ordinance of man; or the exhibition of candles, or the attitudes of the minister, or any other of the thousand questions which have given rise to

---

* " Whilst the clergy are wrangling on points of doctrine, Infidelity is advancing nearer and nearer its strongholds, and taking possession of the mind of the people. The state of the population is not such as to warrant them in wasting their energies on subjects that are left undecided, instead of applying themselves to their proper work."—*Extract from the Bishop of Winchester's Charge, delivered August,* 1850.

so much ill feeling between the clergy and their parishioners? It is useful and fitting no doubt, that all shall be done "decently, and in order," but these things have no influence on the salvation of souls, and should be reduced again to their proper position, as civil ordinances of the land we live in,—not questions of vital importance. Let us all rather join heart and hand in the noble work of teaching those sunk in the animal life, the brighter hopes which await them: let us show them that there is a happiness of which they have as yet formed no idea, but which when once felt is not forgotten; and when they have come to that knowledge and felt that happiness, we may safely leave them to their human instincts to pursue it. They and we may then walk together in the steps of our meek and lowly Master through life, and when that is over, share together in his exaltation.

THE END.

C. WHITTINGHAM, CHISWICK.